HERBS

HERBS

1001 Gardening Questions Answered

by
The Editors of Garden Way Publishing

Foreword by Phyllis V. Shaudys

A GARDEN WAY PUBLISHING BOOK

STOREY COMMUNICATIONS, INC.
POWNAL, VERMONT 05261

Produced by Storey Communications, Inc.
President, M. John Storey
Executive Vice President of Administration, Martha M. Storey
Publisher, Thomas Woll

Written by Ann Reilly and the Editors of Garden Way Publishing
Cover and interior design by Andrea Gray
Edited by Gwen W. Steege
Illustrated by Brigita Fuhrmann, except insect drawings, pages
    50-53, by Judy Eliason
Production by Andrea Gray and Rebecca Babbitt
Front cover photograph by Madelaine Gray
Back cover photograph by Derek Fell
Interior photographs by Henry W. Art, Derek Fell, Madelaine Gray,
    Maggie Oster, Positive Images (Jerry Howard, Ivan Massar), Ann
    Reilly, and Ron West
Chapter opening photographs by Madelaine Gray (1), Maggie Oster
    (2, 3), Positive Images, Jerry Howard (4), and Henry W. Art (5).
Map by Northern Cartographic
Typesetting by StereoType & Design, So. Burlington, VT.

Quality Printing and Binding By:
ARCATA GRAPHICS/KINGSPORT
Press and Roller Streets
Kingsport, TN 37662 U.S.A.

Herbs: 1001 gardening questions answered / by the editors of Garden
    Way Publishing; foreword by Phyllis V. Shaudys.

    "A Garden Way Publishing book."
    Includes bibliographical references (p. 142).
    ISBN 0-88266-570-7: $16.95
    1. Herb gardening—Miscellanea.   I. Garden Way Publishing.
SB351.H5H372 1990
635'.7—dc20   89-84635
                                                                        CIP

Contents

In recent years American gardeners have become increasingly enthusiastic about growing their own herbs. In fact, not since the seventeenth and eighteenth centuries, when colonists brought herb seeds from Europe to begin their first gardens in a new homeland, has herb gardening been so popular. Surveys suggest that over six million families spend nearly $50 million each year on this intriguing pastime. For these avid gardeners, *Herbs: 1001 Gardening Questions Answered* provides a wealth of information on successful herb horticulture and care, as well as the practical uses of these fragrant plants.

The renaissance of interest in herbs has resulted in part from a heightened awareness of the healthful benefits of natural foods, as well as the gourmet delights of creative cooking with fresh herbs. Fresh is better—fresh, homegrown without pesticides is better yet! And fresh herbs not only taste better, but unlike many commercially prepared seasonings, they contain no sodium, preservatives, or other additives. In addition, growing and drying herbs makes it possible to create potpourris for natural fragrances or herbal wreaths and arrangements for the "country" look so much in vogue—all of which make welcome additions to your own home or lovely and useful gifts. Whether you raise herbs for stuffing poultry with fresh sage and thyme from the garden or creating unique salt-free seasonings, healthful herbal teas, or seasoned vinegars and oils for an enlightened cuisine; concocting fragrant blends to steep on the stove or in the bath; making herbal decorations to sell at a church bazaar or to decorate a family wedding; or simply because you love fragrant plants—this book will answer most, if not all, questions that might arise.

New herb growers especially will enjoy Chapter 5, "Favorite Herbs to Grow"—an overview of the most popular herbs, along with detailed plant descriptions, cultural requirements, past and present uses, and even some fascinating lore. This will help you decide which herbs to begin with, dependent upon your tastes, needs, and climate. When you are ready to purchase your seeds or plants, be sure to use the Latin (or botanical) names given in this chapter to accurately identify your selections. When plotting your first herb garden—or planning where to fit herbs into your existing perennial or vegetable gardens—you can consult the comprehensive herb charts in the appendix to coordinate plant heights, necessary exposures, and soil requirements with your own situation.

During the last thirty years I have read extensively about herbs, published a national newsletter on herbs, and experimented with growing almost every kind of herb suitable for my Pennsylvania climate, yet I still feel that this book adds much useful information to what currently exists in books on the subject. For example, I think many gardeners will be interested to learn how soil acidity or alkalinity affects different herbs and how treating the soil can give better results. Equally helpful are the explanations for why some herbs thrive in one part of the country but not in another—why angelica, for instance, thrives in Seattle and why chamomile doesn't do well in Nashville. This and other information combine to provide an essential reference book for both experienced and novice gardeners. I recommend this book for your personal library and thoughtful study. And I wish each reader much joy and pleasure in your experiences with the useful and delightful herbs in your garden.

Derek Fell

Phyllis V. Shaudys
Author, *The Pleasure of Herbs*

HERBS

1 *Gardening with Herbs*

The subtle colors, pungent and heady fragrances, dependability, variety of usages, and legendry of herbs has, for centuries, made them endlessly fascinating to gardeners everywhere. Any spot of sunshine can become home for an herb garden, whether that "garden" is a single flower pot or an intricately fashioned, Elizabethan-style knot garden.

Although botanists define herbs as plants that die down over winter rather than form woody stems, most gardeners and cooks recognize herbs for their medicinal, flavorful, or aromatic qualities. It is well known that a sprinkling of a few herbs magically and healthfully seasons and enhances cooked foods, but herbs are equally delicious in teas, butters, jellies, garnishes, and vinegars. Their uses extend beyond the kitchen to flower arrangements, sachets and potpourris, soaps and cosmetics, dyes, and insect repellents.

As the multifaceted world of herbs, and their culture, history, and usages open up to you in the chapters that follow, the pleasures of growing herbs will enrich your garden as well as your kitchen, and indeed your whole house.

What is the difference between an herb and a spice?

Because spices, like herbs, season or flavor food, it is clear that the differences between the two are subtle and overlapping. Some consider that herbs come from leaves and seeds, and spices come from fruit, roots, bark, and berries, but the roots of some herbs are useful, as are the leaves of some spices. Others classify temperate-climate plants as herbs and tropical plants as

◆ *Herb gardens, no matter how large or small, are endlessly fascinating to gardeners everywhere.*

1

spices. Yet others regard spices as more flavorful or hotter to the taste than herbs. At best, the definitions and differences are subtle.

What is the proper way to pronounce the word "herb"?

Either "urb" or "hurb" is correct. In the United States, the pronunciation is usually "urb"; in England, "hurb." American and British pronunciations of the word *basil* differ also, with Americans generally saying "bayzle," and British, "bazzle."

What is an "Herbal"?

Written as early as the fifteenth century, herbals were books that described the plants known in earlier times. This history, lore, and legend of plants that we still enjoy growing today continues to make fascinating reading.

Are herbs annuals, biennials, or perennials?

There are annual, biennial, and perennial herbs. An annual flowers, sets seed, and dies all in one year. A biennial flowers, sets seed, and dies over two years. A perennial lives from year to year, usually flowering and setting seed in spring and summer, dying to the ground in winter, and regrowing the following spring.

You list fennel, scented geranium, lemon grass, marjoram, and rosemary as perennials, but I thought they were annuals. Can you explain?

These herbs are not winter hardy in cold climates and are therefore grown in most parts of the country as annuals, although technically they are perennials.

Will you please explain the terms "winter hardy" and "hardiness zone"?

The U.S. Department of Agriculture has divided the United States and Canada into ten hardiness zones, based on the average minimum winter temperature in each area. Every perennial has been assigned a hardiness zone through which it will survive the winter outdoors. You should check the hardiness of each perennial herb you are planning to add to the garden to determine if it will grow in your area. When a plant is said to be not "winter hardy," it means it will not tolerate frost.

I have read that parsley is a biennial. Can't it be harvested the first year?

Actually, parsley is *best* harvested the first year. Although technically it is a biennial, because it does not flower until its second year, after it flowers it produces few—and bitter—leaves.

COMMON ANNUAL AND BIENNIAL HERBS

angelica
anise
basil
borage
calendula
caraway
chamomile (German)
chervil
clary
coriander
cumin
dill
fennel
garlic
lemon grass
lemon verbena
marjoram
oregano
parsley
pennyroyal (American)
perilla
rosemary
safflower
scented geraniums
sesame
summer savory
watercress

Parsley, a biennial, stays fresh and green even in very cold fall weather, but the leaves it produces the following spring are bitter.

Which other herbs are biennials? Can any be grown as annuals?

Angelica, caraway, clary, and watercress are biennials. If you are growing angelica and watercress for their leaves, which can be harvested at any time, they can be grown as annuals. Caraway is grown for its seeds, and it will not flower and set seeds until the second year. Clary, if grown for its foliage, can be grown as an annual, but it will not flower until the second year.

COMMON PERENNIAL HERBS

anise hyssop	horseradish	saffron
artemisia	hyssop	sage
bee balm	lavender	scented geraniums
burnet	lavender cotton	sweet cicely
catnip	lemon balm	sweet flag
chamomile (Roman)	lemon grass	sweet woodruff
chives	lovage	tansy
comfrey	marjoram	tarragon
costmary	mints	thyme
fennel	oregano	valerian
germander	pennyroyal (English)	winter savory
ginseng	rosemary	yarrow
horehound	rue	

What is meant by a hardy annual? What are some examples?

Hardy annuals are those annual herbs that are not damaged by frost and thus can be planted outdoors in early spring, or even in fall and overwintered. Some hardy annual herbs are anise, borage, calendula, German chamomile, chervil, coriander, dill, garlic (which is actually a bulb, but because the bulb itself is harvested, it is usually grown as an annual or biennial), American pennyroyal, and summer savory.

Why are some herbs called tender annuals?

These are annual herbs that are easily injured by frost and thus must be planted only after the ground has warmed up and all danger of frost is past in spring; they will be killed by the first frost of fall. Examples of these are basil, cumin, perilla, safflower, and sesame.

HERBS FOR SPECIAL PLACES AND PURPOSES

I don't have room for a large herb garden but would like to grow some herbs this year. How might I do this?

Herbs don't need to be grown in a garden by themselves (although they certainly can be if you have the room and the desire). You can mix herbs in flower beds and borders, integrate them in the vegetable garden, grow them in pots, or use them as edgings and borders, depending on their size and growth habits.

Why should I include herbs in my garden design?

The flavor of fresh herbs usually far surpasses that of dried herbs in foods and beverages, and some herbs have pretty flowers that can be enjoyed fresh or used dried, as well. Perhaps one of the greatest pleasures of growing herbs is learning about them, for they have more legend and lore attached to them than possibly any other group of plants.

Is it necessary to have full sun for growing herbs?

No. Many herbs need full sun, but others will grow in partial, or even complete, shade.

My garden is partially shaded, receiving sun for only a few hours in the morning. What herbs can I grow?

In partial shade such as you describe, try catnip, chervil, costmary, germander, horseradish, rosemary, sweet flag, sweet woodruff, or valerian. Mint does best in full sun but will survive (and not be as aggressive) in partial shade.

I'm confused about burnet. Is it a plant for sun or shade?

Burnet prefers full sun, but if it is very hot, it grows better in light shade.

My backyard has very light shade all day, as the sunlight is dappled by nearby trees. What can I plant there?

The herbs mentioned that grow in partial shade might do well in this situation. You could also add angelica, anise hyssop, bee balm, borage, calendula, chamomile, chives, hyssop, lemon balm, lovage, parsley, pennyroyal, perilla, saffron, sage, and tarragon.

Are there any herbs that will grow in a shaded, woodland garden?

Yes, chervil, ginseng, sweet cicely, and sweet woodruff will tolerate heavy shade. Watercress must also be grown in the shade if it is grown in the ground rather than in water.

I have read that herbs must have dry soil. Is this true?

Many herbs need dry soil to produce their most fragrant or flavorful foliage. The ones most demanding of this are anise, bee balm, borage, burnet, caraway, catnip, horehound, hyssop, lavender, lavender cotton, perilla, tarragon, thyme, and yarrow.

My Seattle garden is rarely dry during the summer. What can I grow in my herb garden, which has well-drained soil?

The list has many offerings. You could successfully grow angelica, calendula, chervil, chives, clary, coriander, dill, garlic, horseradish, lemon balm, lemon verbena, mint, pennyroyal, rue, saffron, savory, sweet flag, sweet woodruff, tansy, valerian, and watercress.

Sweet woodruff makes a lovely ground cover in partially shaded areas.

Like the gardener in Seattle, I also have moist soil, but my garden is much colder in the winter. Will the same herbs do well for me?

Yes, and you can add to your list ginseng and lovage plants that actually *require* cold winters, which would not occur in the Seattle area.

Are there any other herbs that must have cold winters to grow well?

Yes, besides ginseng and lovage, English lavender, hyssop, sweet cicely, silver artemisia, tarragon, and yarrow must have freezing temperatures during the winter or they will not grow well.

Chamomile did not grow well in my Nashville garden. What might be wrong?

It is most likely too hot during your summers for chamomile. For the same reason, you may not be able to grow calendula, chervil, parsley, pennyroyal, and watercress in your region. Try growing them in the spring or fall, or substitute other plants.

What herbs will tolerate the high heat of my Texas garden in summer?

The most heat-resistant herbs are angelica, cumin, germander, lemon grass, and sesame.

What does the term "kitchen garden" mean?

This descriptive phrase refers to a fairly small garden composed of edible plants, both vegetable and herb. If possible, it's nice to have such a garden close to the house, handy for last-minute additions to summer meals.

What annual herbs would you suggest for a beginner to grow in a kitchen garden?

The easiest herbs to grow from seed are basil, borage, chervil, chives, dill, parsley (really a biennial but grown as an annual), summer savory, and sweet marjoram.

Small kitchen gardens consist of edible plants, both vegetables and herbs.

Positive Images, Jerry Howard

I have never grown herbs before and would like to plant a few perennial herbs. What would you suggest I start with for a kitchen garden?

Try chives, French tarragon, peppermint, rosemary, sage, spearmint, and thyme. Rosemary will not survive outdoors where winters are below freezing, but it is easy to grow and such an important culinary herb that it should not be excluded from your garden (see pages 109-10). You will probably have greatest success if you purchase plants of all of these (except perhaps chives), rather than starting them from seed.

My mother does not see well, so I would like to plant a fragrant garden for her to enjoy. What should I include?

Many herbs fit this category. You can choose from angelica, catnip, costmary, horehound, hyssop, lavender, lavender cotton, lemon balm, lemon grass, lemon verbena, lovage, marjoram, the mints, rosemary, sage (especially pineapple sage), scented geraniums, southernwood, sweet flag, thyme, valerian, and wormwood.

Which herbs are grown for their seeds? I would like to use some herb seeds in baking bread and cookies.

The seeds of angelica, anise, caraway, coriander, cumin, fennel, lovage, and sesame are used in baking as well as for other purposes. Dill seed is well known as a seasoning for pickled cucumbers.

Which herb leaves are grown for culinary use?

The most common ones are basil, borage (young leaves only), burnet, chervil, chives, dill, fennel, lemon balm, marjoram, mints, oregano, parsley, sage, savory, tarragon, and thyme.

Culinary garden plan: (1) Basil, (2) chervil, (3) chives, (4) dill, (5) fennel, (6) lemon balm, (7) lovage, (8) marjoram, (9) oregano, (10) parsley, (11) sage, (12) spearmint, (13) summer savory, (14) tarragon, (15) thyme.

Maggie Oster

Lavender is among the many herbs attractive to bees, which are further welcomed into this garden by skeps (beehives made of twisted straw).

Which herbs are particularly attractive to bees?

Bee balm, borage, hyssop, lavender, lemon balm, lovage, marjoram, sweet cicely, and thyme.

What consideration should I give to the colored foliage of herbs when designing a garden?

Many herbs have gray foliage that blends well with other landscape plants and can be used as a buffer between plantings. Among these are the artemisias, borage, catnip, chamomile, dittany of Crete (see oregano), horehound, horsemint, lavender, lavender cotton, rue, sage, savory, sweet marjoram, and thyme. For a bright spot of color, plant the red-leafed perilla or purple-leafed basil as contrasts.

Other than color, how can the foliage of herbs enhance my garden?

A balance of foliage texture is also quite attractive. For example, use burnet, caraway, chervil, and dill, with their finely divided foliage, as a striking contrast to coarse-leafed angelica, bee balm, borage, and safflower.

Are there any herbs that make good ground covers?

Yes. Try dittany of Crete, mint, Roman chamomile, rosemary, sweet woodruff, or creeping thyme.

I want to grow herbs for fresh and dried flowers. What should I plant?

Many herbs, including bee balm, borage, calendula, lavender, rosemary, sage, tansy, thyme, valerian, and yarrow, have attractive flowers.

I would like to grow a theme garden of plants I can use to make herbal teas. What should I use?

Teas can be made from bee balm, calendula, chamomile, scented geraniums, ginseng, horehound, lemon balm, lemon grass, mints, sage, and sweet cicely.

What herbs would do well to edge a brick or stone wall?

Try basil, catmint, dwarf lavender, lavender cotton, sage, thyme, and winter savory.

What is a knot garden?

This traditional herb garden consists of low-growing plants or hedges planted in a formal, intricate design that resembles knotted ropes. First known in medieval times, knot gardens were very popular during the Elizabethan era. They require more time and work to plan, establish, and maintain than other herb gardens, but they are uniquely peaceful and serene.

What type of plants are commonly used in knot gardens?

The plants should be low-growing and capable of being closely clipped or sheared. Often, plants of contrasting foliage color are used to make the design more dramatic. You could use dwarf lavender, hyssop, lavender cotton, and rosemary. Germander is a traditional border plant for knot gardens.

I saw a knot garden in a local botanic garden and thought I'd try to duplicate it. Do you have any idea what material might have been sprinkled on the ground between the plants to make the design stand out?

It could have been any colorful material, such as marble chips, pea gravel, broken clay pots, sandstone chips, or redwood bark.

Knot gardens seem to take a lot of plants. What is the best way to plant a knot garden without having to buy a lot of plants in one year?

Start your own small nursery bed, increasing the plants every year by seeds, division, or cuttings. In a few years, you will have enough plants to design your knot garden.

PLANNING YOUR HERB GARDEN

•

▨ Germander (*Teucrium Chamaedrys*)

▦ Hyssop (*Hyssopus officinalis*)

▥ Blue Beauty rue (*Ruta Graveolens*)

☐ Munstead lavender (*Lavandula angustifolia*)

A traditional knot garden pattern constructed in a formal, intricate design that resembles knotted ropes.

Maggie Oster

Knot gardens are composed of low-growing plants of contrasting foliage color.

Which herbs would blend in best with annuals and perennials in flower beds and borders?

Many herbs mix quite nicely into the flower garden, including basil, borage, calendula, chamomile, chives, lavender, lemon balm, parsley, rosemary, rue, sage, and thyme. Some of these add their own blossoms to the flower garden; others contribute attractive contrasting foliage.

What is the difference between a bed and a border?

Beds are plantings that are accessible from all sides and intended to be viewed from all sides, such as a planting in the middle of your lawn. Borders are at the edge of an area, and are approached and viewed from only one side. Examples of borders are those plantings along a fence, driveway, foundation, shrub planting, or hedge.

How wide should I make an edging of thyme and rosemary along a walkway?

Edgings should be in proportion to their surroundings. A very wide edging would not look good along a very short walkway. A good rule of thumb is to make an edging no wider than one-third its length.

How large should beds be?

Again, this depends on the size of the surroundings. Keep herb beds in scale with the rest of the property. Any bed that takes up more than one-third of the area in which it is placed will look out of proportion. The size of the bed also depends on how much time you have to take care of it. If you're a beginner, start small; you can always add to it later. You can grow a lot of herbs in an area 3 to 4 feet square.

I'm planning an herb border against the fence in my backyard. How deep should it be?

Borders, too, should be in proportion to their length. Because they can be worked from one side only, however, they should be no deeper than 5 feet, no matter how long they are, so that maintenance will be possible.

What shape should beds be? Do I have to arrange my herbs in a formal bed?

Not at all. This depends on your taste and the style of your home. Formal beds are square, circular, rectangular, or some other regular shape, and they are usually symmetrical. Informal beds may be round, oval, kidney-shaped, or free-formed.

An herb border frames the edge of an area.

Maggie Oster

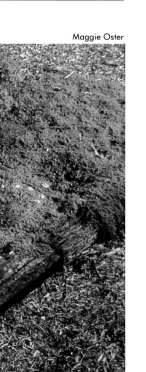

This informal herb bed is enhanced by a sundial placed on a short pedestal.

What are the differences to be considered in designing a formal garden versus an informal one?

Formal gardens, most commonly consisting of straight lines in symmetrical arrangements, should be placed on a flat area with no large trees or shrubs. In contrast, where trees and shrubs are dominant features, it is best to plan an informal, curving garden around these permanent features. Consider both your personal preference and what blends with the style of your house and the rest of your garden.

On a trip to Europe, I saw some formal gardens with interesting designs and liked the effect. How could I recreate this?

Draw a plan to scale on graph paper and then transfer it to the garden bed, using strings or cord to lay it out before you plant. You can create your own original design in the same manner. Start with a square, and place squares, circles, triangles, or other symmetrical forms within it. Dissect the garden diagonally or from side to side with a path if you desire.

Should herb gardens have plants of the same height or varying heights?

That depends on the size of the garden and whether it is formal or informal. In small and formal gardens, low-growing

Formal gardens consist of symmetrically arranged patterns.

plants look best. In large, informal gardens, a variety of heights makes the planting more interesting. Place tall plants in the background, with intermediate-sized plants in front of them, and a low-growing herb as a border. Combine angelica, dill, fennel, lemon verbena, lovage, and southernwood, which are tall plants, with medium-sized anise, borage, oregano, rue, sage, or sweet cicely. Border the garden with basil, chamomile, parsley, or thyme.

Where can I locate herb beds and borders in my garden?

Anywhere where the light and soil conditions are right. Line your walkways or driveway, place a bed right outside the back door or in the middle of the backyard, or a border by the patio or along a fence. When deciding where to put your herb beds and borders, consider the points from which they will be viewed. If you want to see an herb bed from near the dining room, locate it near those windows. If you want to see it from the patio, that's where it should be. If the beds or borders contain mostly culinary herbs, place them near the vegetable garden or the kitchen.

Can I situate an herb garden on a slope?

Absolutely! Because water runs off them more quickly, slopes are often dry, and thus ideal for many herbs, especially those

Maggie Oster

Vegetables and herbs are natural companions.

Companion garden plan: (1) Summer savory, (2) asparagus, (3) tomatoes and basil, (4) peppers, (5) marigolds, (6) green beans, (7) summer squash and nasturtiums, (8) lettuce and onions, (9) chives.

that prefer dry soil. Choose low-growing herbs for the best visual effect.

I would like to put plants around the spokes of an old wagon wheel. How would you suggest doing this?

A wagon or oxcart wheel can be made the central feature of a small, formal herb garden. Select a level spot. Place the hub down into the ground and put a few plants of each variety between the spokes. Low-growing, compact plants, such as basil, chamomile, chervil, chives, coriander, hyssop, lemon balm, marjoram, parsley, and savory would be better than tall, scraggly ones.

Can I plant herbs among my vegetables?

Yes, in fact, many herbs, such as artemisia, chives, and thyme, are thought to repel insects that prey on certain vegetables. Be careful to choose herbs that tolerate fertilizer and water, since you will probably be feeding and watering your vegetable garden regularly. Chives and parsley can make decorative edgings in a vegetable garden. If your vegetable garden has raised beds with permanent paths, creeping thyme would make a lovely ground cover on the paths. Dill will grow and show off among squash, but is said to inhibit the growth of tomatoes. If you grow dill with cucumbers, the seeds will be at hand when it comes time for pickling. A few calendula plants add color and are said to repel asparagus beetles.

How can I extend the season for harvesting fresh herbs?

There are several ways. Perennial herbs are often harvestable before annual herbs. If you begin plants indoors by seed, you can set annual plants out earlier than normal in spring, and if

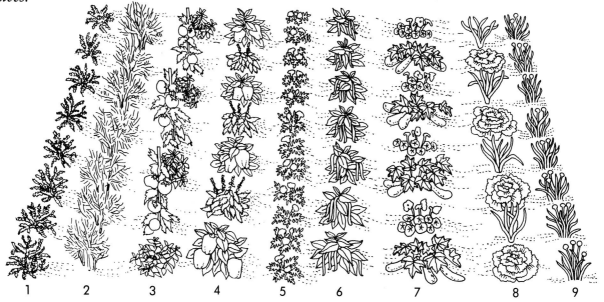

| 1 | 2 | 3 | 4 | 5 | 6 | 7 | 8 | 9 |

frost threatens, protect them with hot caps (plastic or paper tents made to protect young plants from wind and cold) or other covering. In fall, dig some herbs and move them into the cold frame for additional months of harvesting. The ultimate in extending the season, of course, is to grow herbs indoors.

I have a very small garden but I do want to grow a few herbs. What do you suggest?

If you have run out of space in the ground, try growing herbs in containers.

Which herbs grow best in containers?

Anise, basil, chervil, coriander, lavender, lavender cotton, lemon balm, parsley, rosemary, sage, scented geraniums, and summer savory. Edge containers with creeping varieties of chamomile or thyme, which will cascade over the sides.

Where can I place containers?

Containers can be used anywhere that the sun/shade conditions of the plants are met—on patios, porches, decks, balconies, along the walkway, at the front door. To take care of them most easily, be sure they are within reach of the garden hose.

What types of containers other than clay pots might be used for herbs set out on the terrace or sun deck?

Wooden tubs are ideal. Use an old butter tub if you can find one, or purchase redwood or pressure-treated pine planters. Plastic pots are durable and the soil in them stays moist longer than in clay pots. Avoid metal containers as these tend to get too hot.

Which herbs can I grow indoors? I'd like to have fresh herbs for cooking over the winter.

Basil, chives, marjoram, parsley, and rosemary are the best culinary herbs to grow indoors in the winter. Rosemary will need a cool (55° F.) spot in the house. Scented geraniums also do well inside if you want foliage for teas. For all these plants, provide a sunny window or gardening lights.

Is it better to buy seeds and plants from the local garden center or from mail-order catalogs?

Each has advantages. Mail-order catalogs usually have a larger selection and a more complete description of the individual varieties. Garden centers are good for last-minute purchases. Be sure to order or buy seeds early, especially herbs that need to be started indoors. If you order early you will also avoid the disappointment of finding an herb sold out.

Container-grown rosemary does well outdoors in hot, sunny weather, but must be wintered indoors in cold-weather regions.

Maggie Oster

2 *The Basics of Growing Herbs*

Herb seedlings can be purchased, of course, but for many reasons you may wish to start your own plants from seeds. Old favorites, less common herbs, and unusual varieties might not be available as plants. Growing plants from seed is also more economical, a serious consideration if you have a large garden. Plus, starting plants from seeds can be fun!

Why should I start seeds indoors rather than simply sowing seeds into the garden in spring?

Some herb seeds can be sown into the garden but others, because they have a long growing season, will not flower and produce seeds if you do not provide the extended season obtained by starting them indoors. Others may not need to be started indoors, but will flower or be ready for harvest much earlier if they are. Plants with fine seeds should be started indoors as they can easily wash away in the rain outside or they will have a difficult time competing with weeds when they are young.

What are the herbs that I should start inside?

You should start seeds of cumin, germander, lemon balm, rosemary, savory, sesame, valerian, wormwood, and yarrow indoors, or buy plants. Savory, wormwood, and yarrow have fine seeds; the others have such a long growing season that they need a head start indoors. Many others can be started indoors if you so desire.

◄ *Basil will be ready for harvest much earlier if seeds are begun indoors.*

INDOOR SEED PROPAGATION
·

Because the seeds of winter savory are so fine, it is best to sow them indoors.

Are there any herbs that should *not* be started indoors?

Borage, caraway, and horehound should not be started indoors, because they do not transplant well.

Are there any herbs that cannot be grown from seeds?

Yes, usually because they don't set seeds and thus must be propagated from cuttings or division. These include costmary, horseradish, lemon grass, lemon verbena, saffron, French tarragon, and English thyme, a variety of culinary thyme.

Are there examples of herbs that can be grown from seed, but would be better propagated by another method?

Yes, some are difficult to germinate or take a long time to become established from seed, and others do not come true (are not exactly like the parent plant) or are not flavorful from seed. Herbs that are better propagated by division or cuttings include scented geraniums, germander, ginseng, lavender, most mints, oregano, pennyroyal, rosemary, some sages, sweet woodruff, and valerian.

When should I start seeds of annual herbs indoors?

That depends on several factors. The first thing to determine is whether the herb is a hardy annual or a tender annual (see chart on pages 130-31). Hardy annual plants can be set into the garden in mid-spring, while tender annual herbs must not go outdoors until all danger of frost has passed. Once the planting date has been determined, back up six to eight weeks for most herbs, and start the seeds then.

When should I start seeds of biennial herbs indoors?

Since many biennial herbs are grown as annuals, the seeds are usually started indoors in late winter and the plants moved outside in mid-spring, so the plants can be harvested the same year. As an alternative, seeds can be sown either indoors or outdoors over the summer, and seedlings moved to their permanent place in the garden in early fall for harvesting the second year.

When should I start seeds of perennial herbs indoors?

Perennials are treated in much the same way as biennials (see previous questions). They can be started indoors any time from spring through summer and transplanted into the garden at least six weeks before the first fall frost.

What are the basic requirements for starting seeds indoors?

You will need a sterile sowing medium (page 20), steady moisture (page 24), adequate sunlight or fluorescent lights (page 24), suitable temperature (page 25).

Containers and Soil for Indoor Propagation

What kind of container should I use to start seeds indoors?

Traditionally, seeds are started in flats or pots. However, many other specially designed units, modifications of the traditional system, are sold today for the purpose of helping to simplify the process, especially for beginners. Look for trays containing six or more compressed blocks of a special peat-based growing mixture into which you sow one or two seeds per block. Another popular variant is the Jiffy-7—a flat, peat-moss wafer when dry; when moistened, it expands to form a small, filled pot into which a seed or seeds are sown. The wafers are usually placed side by side in a flat or other container. Large seeds can be sown one to a wafer and the plants that result are left to grow until ready to be transplanted outdoors. Small seeds are usually sown several to a pot and transplanted once before being set outdoors.

Commercial growers sometimes now use special flats formed into cone-shaped compartments that are filled with germinating medium. One or two seeds are placed in each compartment, so that after germination the seedlings can become well established in their growing "plug." The advantage of this method is that transplanting shock is minimized; the disadvantage is that you have wasted space if all the seeds do not germinate.

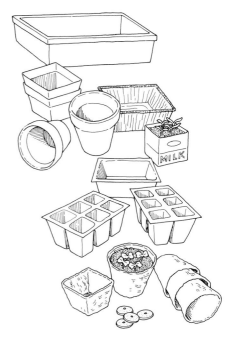

Purchased flats and peat pots, as well as a variety of other containers, are suitable for beginning seedlings indoors.

What is a flat?

It is a shallow, topless box, usually about 3 inches deep, with slits or holes in the bottom to allow for drainage of water from the sowing medium. It can be used for seed germination, as well as for propagating by cuttings. Shallow flats without drainage holes should be avoided because the sowing medium can too easily become waterlogged, or equally bad, dry out too quickly. Use aluminum foil pans, cut-down milk cartons, or other discarded kitchen containers as flats, and punch drainage holes in the bottoms.

Is there any rule about the dimensions of flats?

A great variety of flat sizes is acceptable, as long as the flat is not less than 2½ inches, or more than 4 inches deep. If the dimensions are greater than 14 x 20 inches, the flat is likely to be too heavy to carry comfortably.

Are there advantages to using flats made of compressed fiber?

Yes, but disadvantages too. Compressed fiber flats are very porous, which ensures good aeration and lessens the chance of overwatering. However, they dry out very quickly and must thus be constantly watched. Do not reuse these flats as they are not sterile after their first use.

Are there any special techniques necessary when using fiber or peat flats or pots?

Yes, make sure these containers are completely soaked in water before you fill them with medium and sow your seeds or the container will act as a wick and pull moisture from the medium.

Are individual pots or Jiffy-7s ever particularly advantageous for sowing seeds?

Some seedlings, such as anise, dill, fennel, lovage, parsley, perilla, safflower, savory, sesame, and sweet cicely, do not transplant well. If you plant them in individual pots you will not disturb their roots when you move them into the garden.

How many flats should I plan on? I have never started seeds indoors before.

You can safely estimate that a flat 5 ½ x 7 ½ inches will hold 100 seedlings of large seeds, 200 seedlings of medium seeds, and 300 seedlings of fine seeds.

Should I sow more seeds than I need?

Definitely! Not all of the seeds will germinate, and some will be lost in transplanting. If you have extra plants, you can share them with your neighbors and friends.

What sowing medium is preferable for seeds sown indoors?

It is best to use a soilless mix such as half sand, perlite, or vermiculite and half peat moss. The most convenient material is a prepared, sterile mix sold for this purpose and containing sufficient nutrients to carry seedlings through until transplanting time. If grown indoors in garden soil, seeds do not germinate well, and a fungus disease called damping off (see page 53) is common.

I have never started seeds indoors before. How much sowing medium will I need?

You can estimate that 4 cups of medium will be needed for each 5½ x 7½-inch flat.

I filled my flats with sowing medium and then watered the medium prior to sowing. But all the perlite floated to the top, and the medium didn't moisten evenly. What went wrong?

The medium must be moistened before it is placed into the flats. Put it in a large bowl or plastic bag to moisten it. Use about 1½ cups of water for every 4 cups of medium.

How should I go about sowing seeds of herbs indoors in a flat?

Cover the drainage holes in containers with moss or pieces of broken flower pot; follow with an inch of flaky leafmold or peat moss; fill with moistened sowing medium to within ¼ inch of the top of the flat; press down level and sow the seeds.

How deep should seeds be planted in flats and pots indoors?

Indoors, very small seeds are firmly pressed into the soil with a tamper or covered with a dusting of fine soil, sand, or vermiculite; medium-sized seeds are covered ⅛ to ¼ inch deep; large seeds, about two to three times their diameter.

What is a tamper?

Used for tamping soil firmly in flats, a tamper is an oblong piece of board with a handle attached (similar to a mason's float). If you don't have one, the base of a tumbler or small flowerpot can be used.

I sowed seeds of wormwood indoors last year and did not cover them with medium because they were very fine. However, germination was poor. What did I do wrong?

Fine seeds must be in contact with the moistened medium to germinate. It is possible that you were unsuccessful because the seeds were caught in a small air pocket when they were sown. After sowing fine seeds, gently press them into the medium, or water them with a very fine spray of water to ensure that they are touching the medium. A rubber bulb sprinkler is the best way to do this, as the spray of water is very fine and will not dislodge the seedlings.

Can seed flats be reused from year to year?

Yes, plastic or foil flats can be reused because they can be thoroughly cleaned to prevent transmission of disease. Those made of compressed peat or fiber should not be reused, however, as they cannot be cleaned properly.

How should I clean flats before reusing them?

To prevent damping off and other diseases, disinfect flats by washing them thoroughly with soap and water and rinsing them in a 10-percent solution of bleach in water.

Can I reuse sowing medium?

No, you should not reuse sowing medium for germinating seeds, as it may not be sterile. You can use it, however, for transplants, container plants, and houseplants.

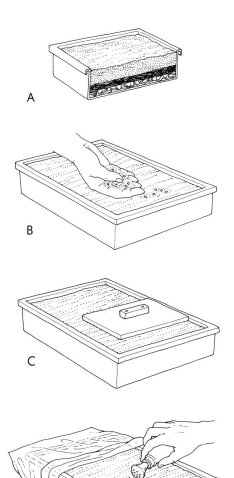

(A) Layer broken pottery, peat moss, and moistened sowing medium in flat before sowing seeds; (B) mix very fine seeds with a bit of sand to ensure more even broadcasting; (C) press seeds into soil with a tamper; (D) gently moisten seed bed with a rubber bulb sprinkler and cover flat with plastic.

Are there any rules about which types of seeds to sow together? I want to grow several types of seedlings in the same flat.

Yes, combine those seeds that need the same temperature and light conditions to germinate, and that will germinate in the same length of time.

Is it better to scatter the seeds or to sow them in rows?

When flats are used, it is preferable to sow them in rows. You can judge germination better, cultivate lightly without danger of harming seedlings, and transplant with more ease. To sow seeds, hold the seed packet between your thumb and third finger and tap gently with your forefinger to distribute the seed.

How can very small seeds be sown evenly?

You may find it easier to broadcast very fine seeds, as they are often difficult to sow in rows. Mix them thoroughly with sand before sowing.

Is it a good idea to sow all of my seeds?

No, save a few, just in case something goes wrong and you have to start over.

Valerian seeds are short lived and must be used only when fresh.

Maggie Oster

What other accessories will I need to get seeds to germinate indoors?

So you don't need to rely on your memory, use labels to record the type of plant and the sowing date. Also keep a record book to help you next year in deciding which herb seeds to buy, how long it took for the seeds to germinate, whether you started them too early or too late, and whether you grew too few or too many of a particular plant.

I saved seeds from last year. Is there any way to tell if they are still good before I sow them?

Yes, take ten seeds and place them in a moist paper towel. Place the paper towel in a plastic bag. Set it in a warm spot (unless it is an herb that likes cool temperatures to germinate). Check the chart on pages 132-33 to see how many days are normally required for germination. After that time, start looking at the seeds. If eight or more have germinated, the seeds are fine. If five to eight have germinated, sow more heavily than usual. If fewer than five have germinated, you won't have good results. Fewer than two, don't use them at all.

Are there any herbs whose seeds can't be saved from year to year?

Yes, some have short-lived seeds that must be used only when they are fresh. These include angelica, anise, lovage, and valerian.

Caring for Herb Seedlings Indoors

After I sow my seeds, how should I treat the flats?

It is important to keep humidity high around a seed flat so seeds will germinate properly. Slip your flats into a clear plastic bag or cover them with a pane of glass until germination occurs to keep humidity at its proper level. Once seeds have germinated, remove the plastic or glass. This technique will also eliminate the need for watering, which may dislodge the seeds during the germination period.

I placed my flats in plastic bags and then noticed a great deal of condensation inside. Was I right to remove the flats from the bag for a few hours to let the medium dry out?

Probably, although condensation can be caused by a change in room temperature and does not necessarily mean the flats are too wet. If the medium appears quite wet, however, allow the flat to dry out a little before placing it in the plastic bag.

How much light is needed during germination?

That depends on the type of seed you are sowing. Since more seeds must be completely covered with sowing medium because they require darkness to germinate, they do not need to receive any special light until after they have germinated, when they must be moved onto a sunny windowsill or under fluorescent lights. Other seeds *require* light to germinate. These seeds should not be covered with medium and must be placed in good light.

Which herb seeds need darkness to germinate?

The list includes borage, calendula, coriander, fennel, and parsley.

When starting seeds in the house in the winter, how do you keep plants short and stocky, not tall and spindly?

A combination of good light, moderate temperature, and avoidance of overcrowding will encourage short, stocky growth. Turn the pots daily to keep the plants from "drawing" to the light. If your windows supply insufficient light, use fluorescent lights.

When should herb seeds be planted in seed flats under fluorescent lights?

Most seedlings require six to eight weeks of growth time indoors before being transplanted into the garden. The timing is the same whether the seedlings are grown under fluorescent light or on a windowsill, provided the window supplies enough light.

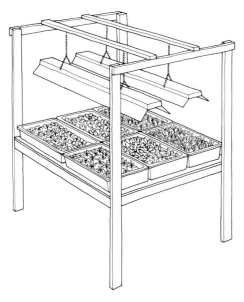

An adjustable fluorescent light unit can be raised as the plants grow.

Do any seedlings require more than six to eight weeks indoors?

Germander, lemon balm, and valerian will require ten to twelve weeks of growing time indoors before they can be transplanted.

What fluorescent unit is best for starting seeds under lights?

The most commonly sold unit consists of two 20-watt fluorescent tubes 2 feet long. This is enough light for most seedlings until they reach a sufficient size for planting outdoors. However, for superior results and to get flowering of many herbs (as well as houseplants) indoors, use a larger unit. The most popular setup is a unit consisting of four 40-watt fluorescent tubes 4 feet long. The light unit should be adjustable so that it can be raised or lowered according to the needs of the plants. When the plants are small, set the lights about 3 inches above them, and then gradually raise the unit as the plants grow.

How can I tell if my seedlings are receiving the proper amount of light?

If the plants show signs of burning, the lights should be raised. If seedlings are growing tall and spindly, they are not receiving enough light, and the lights should be lowered.

Should I leave fluorescent lights on constantly or should plants have a dark period?

For growing seedlings, the lights are generally left on for twenty-four hours until the seeds germinate. After that, leave them on during the day from fourteen to sixteen hours. A time clock is a great convenience in turning the lights on and off.

What are the advantages of growing seedlings under fluorescent light as compared to growing them in a sunny window?

Fluorescent units give a steady supply of light at all times. Because of cloudy days and the low intensity and short duration of winter light, natural light from a window is often inadequate.

How should seed flats be watered after the seed is sown?

Water thoroughly after seeding with a fine overhead spray from a watering can or a bulb-type or mist sprinkler until the soil is saturated. Subsequently, water when the surface soil shows signs of dryness. The medium should be constantly moist but never soggy. It is important not to overwater, but also not to permit the flat to dry out.

Many growers prefer to put the entire flat in a larger pan containing about 1 inch of water, as there is less danger of washing out fine seeds. Do not leave the flat in water any longer

To water seed flats without risk of washing away soil, place flat in a larger container of water, filled to a depth of about 1 inch.

than necessary for moisture to show on the surface, and do not submerge the flat so water washes in and displaces the seeds.

When should I start to fertilize my seedlings?

Start fertilizing once the first set of true leaves has developed (the first leafy growth you will see are *cotyledons*, which are food storage cells, and not true leaves). Use a soluble plant food at one-quarter label strength at first, gradually increasing to full strength as the plants mature.

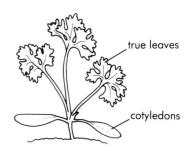

The lower leaves are called seed leaves or cotyledons.

Why do seedlings begun in the house grow to about an inch, bend over, and die?

This is due to damping off, a fungus disease. Prevent it by germinating seeds in sterile medium only, thinning seedlings properly, not overwatering, and giving seedlings fresh air without drafts.

I have heard that parsley seeds should be soaked before being sown. Why is this?

Parsley seeds are very slow to germinate. Soaking them in warm water before sowing them speeds up the time for germination. Cover the seeds two to three times their depth in water. Soak them for twenty-four hours, changing the water several times. When the soaking period is over, sow the seeds immediately and do not allow them to dry out.

I have had problems germinating angelica and anise seeds indoors. What might be the cause?

Seeds of some herbs, including angelica, ginseng, lavender, and sweet cicely, require a chilling before they are sown. This process is known as *stratification*. Seeds must also be moist during the chilling, so do not chill them in the seed packet. Mix the seeds with moistened sowing medium, using about two to three times as much medium as you have seeds, and place them in the refrigerator for the necessary time period. (See the specific plant listings in Chapter 5.)

Can seeds be stratified outdoors?

Yes, you can prechill your seeds outdoors, provided the temperature is constantly below 40° F. for at least the necessary chilling period. Seeds can be presown in flats and placed outdoors for the necessary time, or sown directly into the ground in fall for germination the following spring.

What temperatures do seeds need to germinate properly indoors?

Most seeds require a temperature of 70° F. within the medium. (See next questions.)

Ann Reilly

Watercress seeds require a cool room for germination.

What seeds require a cool room for germination?

Bee balm, chamomile, coriander, rosemary, thyme, and watercress require a cool room, about 55° to 60° F. An unheated sun room, attic, or basement might be the perfect place.

I keep my house very cool in winter. What can I do to give my seeds the warmth they need to germinate?

Apply bottom heat to the seedling flats during the germination period. Your garden center should supply heating cables or heating trays, which you place under the flats to keep them warm. Some have a thermostat that automatically keeps the flats at the proper temperature. If the heating cable doesn't have a thermostat, use a soil thermometer to make sure the temperature is right.

Instead of heating cables, it is usually warm enough on the top of the refrigerator to germinate seeds. Once the seeds have germinated, move them from this spot into good light so they will grow properly.

Will heating cables be needed during the summer to germinate seeds?

No, probably not, unless your house is air conditioned.

Is there any way I can prevent seedlings begun indoors from too-rapid growth and decline?

Too-high temperatures and too early a start often account for the conditions described.

What is the proper method of transplanting seedlings indoors?

First, water the seedlings well. Next, prepare the cells or pots and fill them with moistened medium, making a hole in the center into which the seedlings will be placed. Gently lift the seedling from the flat using a spoon handle or similar tool. To eliminate the possibility of breaking the stem, always handle the seedlings by their leaves, never by the stems. Lower the seedling into the hole and gently press the medium around the roots.

After I transplanted my seedlings, they wilted. What should I have done?

Wilting is normal after transplanting. Place the newly transplanted seedlings in good light, but not full sun, for a few days before returning them to full light. If transplants are severely wilted, place them in a plastic bag or mist them regularly until they recover.

Do seedlings need to be pinched back after being transplanted?

Some, especially angelica, basil, borage, mint, perilla, and scented geraniums, benefit from pinching at this point. Any other seedlings that are growing too tall can be pinched to keep them from becoming too leggy. Simply reach into the center of the plant with your fingers and pinch out the growing tip. Removing the growing shoot in this manner encourages branching.

How do you make new plants blossom earlier in the season?

There is not much that can be done to make herbs bloom early unless they are forced in a greenhouse. Most plants have to reach a certain age before they will flower.

Can I transfer my seedlings directly to the garden from the flat in which they were sown?

This is generally not a good practice unless the seeds were sown in individual pots or cells. Once two sets of true leaves have developed, it is best to transplant seedlings into individual cells or pots so their roots can develop properly and not be subject to transplanting shock later on.

What is the best mixture for transplanting seedlings from flats into pots?

You can use a mixture of 50-percent good garden soil, 25-percent organic matter, and 25-percent perlite, vermiculite, or sharp sand, or a potting mixture, which can be purchased at local garden centers.

THE FIRST TRANSPLANTING OF HERB SEEDLINGS

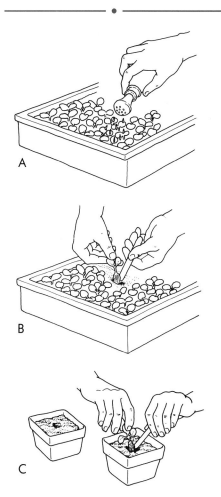

To transplant young seedlings, (A) water well; (B) lift seedling with a spoon handle; and, (C) holding leaves, lower seedling into the hole and firm soil well.

Pinch the growing tip to encourage branching.

OUTDOOR SEED PROPAGATION

If you have little room in your house to start seedlings indoors, most herbs that can be grown from seed can be started right in the garden. The exceptions are cumin, lemon balm, germander, rosemary, sesame, valerian, wormwood, and yarrow. On the other hand, borage, caraway, and horehound *must* be started in the garden. Others that do well started outside include anise, dill, fennel, lovage, parsley, perilla, safflower, sesame, and sweet cicely.

What should the temperature be before herbs are planted in the garden?

There is no set temperature. Most perennial, biennial, and hardy annual herb seeds can be sown as soon as the ground is ready to work, and tender annuals can be started when all danger of frost is past for the region.

Can I start seeds of biennial and perennial herbs outdoors during the summer?

Yes, as long as they are started early enough to germinate and grow large enough by the first fall frost to carry them over the winter.

Which herbs can I sow outdoors in early spring?

Borage (upper left) can be sown in the fall to germinate the following spring; chamomile (right) should be sown outdoors in early spring as soon as the soil can be worked.

As soon as your soil can be worked, sow anise, bee balm, calendula, chamomile, dill, horehound, rosemary, rue, summer savory, tansy, and thyme.

Madelaine Gray

Are there herb seeds that I can plant outdoors in the fall?

Yes. Angelica, borage, hyssop, lavender, lemon balm, lovage, and sweet cicely can be sown in the fall to germinate the following spring. Caraway can be sown early in the fall so it will germinate in the fall and be ready for harvest the following season. Parsley can be sown and germinated in the fall and harvested in the spring in mild-winter areas.

How can I tell when my soil is ready to be worked?

To test the soil for readiness, take a handful and squeeze it. If it stays together in a ball, it is too wet and should not be worked. When you work in too wet soil, you push the air out of it, compacting it so that when it dries it is rock hard and ruined for planting purposes until it is retilled. Wait a few days and try again. When the soil crumbles, it is ready.

I have purchased a self-ventilating cold frame. When can I sow herb seeds in it?

These solar-powered frames usually open automatically when the temperature reaches around 70° F. and close when it drops to 68° F. In most northern areas, perennials, biennials, and hardy annuals can be sown into them in March or early April, and tender annuals a few weeks later.

What does this mean: "Sow seeds when the maple leaves are expanding?"

The unfolding of the maple leaves in the spring indicates that the season has sufficiently advanced to sow perennial, biennial, and hardy annual seeds outdoors.

Preparing the Outdoor Seedbed

How should I prepare my outdoor seedbeds? I am putting in an herb garden for the first time.

Remove the grass and any stones or debris that are in the soil. With a spade or fork, turn the soil over to a depth of 12 inches. Many herbs, such as anise, burnet, caraway, dill, fennel, lovage, parsley, and sweet cicely, have a deep tap root, and the soil should be prepared as deep as the roots will grow. Perennial beds should be well prepared so the plants do not need to be disturbed unless they are divided or transplanted. If you have a tiller, this will make the job easier.

Can I plant my herb garden in the same spot every year?

As long as the soil is well prepared each year and organic matter and fertilizer are added when it is necessary, there is nothing wrong with the practice. However, those herbs that are prone to root rot, such as anise, dill, fennel, sage, and thyme, and aster yellows, such as caraway, chamomile, dill, parsley, and sage, should be rotated each year to avoid these soil-borne disease problems.

What type of soil and what fertilizing programs are best for herbs?

That varies with the herb: Some like soil that is rich in organic matter, such as compost or peat moss; others have the best fragrance and flavor if little organic matter is present. Likewise, some herbs do better if the soil is not fertilized. See the following questions for general advice or refer to Chapter 5 for information about specific herbs. Most herbs will thrive in average garden soil that is well-drained and rather light rather than claylike.

Which herbs grow best in soil that has little organic matter?

Anise hyssop, bee balm, borage, burnet, catmint, catnip, chamomile, costmary, horehound, lavender cotton, lemon balm, oregano, rue, savory, sweet woodruff, thyme, and yarrow should receive no organic matter when preparing the soil.

Which herbs should be grown in soil to which organic matter has been added?

Calendula, chervil, chives, clary, ginseng, horseradish, lemon verbena, lovage, mint, parsley, pennyroyal, perilla, saffron, sweet cicely, sweet flag, sweet woodruff, tansy, tarragon, and valerian like generous amounts of organic matter (at least 25 percent of the soil volume), such as compost, peat moss, or leaf mold, when preparing the soil. For other herbs, add moderate amounts of organic matter (about 10 to 15 percent of the final soil volume).

Should I incorporate fertilizer into the soil before planting?

Except for those herbs that should not be fertilized, add a small amount of complete fertilizer, such as 4-12-4 or 5-10-5, before planting, or in the spring when growth starts. Further fertilizing during the year will rarely be necessary. Tarragon should receive no chemical fertilizer, but likes to be fed with fish emulsion. Fresh animal manures will cause rust on mints and oregano.

How much fertilizer should I use?

That depends on the type of fertilizer and the herb. As a general rule, for those herbs that require fertilizer, you can estimate using 1 pound of 5-10-5 fertilizer per 100 square feet on a new bed and ½ pound per 100 square feet on an established bed. Read the fertilizer label for detailed instructions.

Maggie Oster

Lavender cotton and thyme grow best in soil that has little organic matter.

What do the numbers 5-10-5 mean?

The numbers refer to the percentages of nitrogen, phosphorus, and potassium (NPK) present in the fertilizer. A bag of 5-10-5 contains 5-percent nitrogen, 10-percent phosphorus, and 5-percent potassium; the remaining 80 percent is inert filler. Nitrogen is necessary for foliage and stem growth; phosphorus, for root development and flower production; potassium, for plant metabolism and the production of food.

What is slow-release fertilizer? Can it be used on herbs?

Slow-release fertilizer is a special type of fertilizer that is inactive until released by water or temperature. The three- or six-month formulation works very well on herbs. Apply in early to mid-spring; no additional feedings will be necessary.

I like to apply liquid fertilizer to my flower and vegetable garden during the summer. Should I feed my herbs at the same time?

With the possible exception of scented geraniums and those herbs that are grown for their flowers, application of liquid fertilizer during the summer would provide too rich an environment for herbs.

What sort of amendments should I add to the soil to improve its texture?

If drainage is poor, add perlite, vermiculite, gypsum, or coarse sand. The addition of organic matter such as peat moss, leaf

31

mold, or compost depends on the type of herb you will be growing. These materials enrich as well as improve the texture of soil, and as has been noted, some herbs do better in soil that has no added organic matter.

I hear a lot about soil pH. What is it, and need I be concerned about it when I grow herbs?

The pH is a measurement of the relative acidity and alkalinity of soil on a scale of 1 to 14. Most herbs like a pH of 6.0 to 7.0, which is slightly acid to neutral. You can test your garden soil with a soil test kit available at your local garden center, or have it tested by your county extension service agent. If the pH needs to be raised, use lime; if it needs to be lowered, use sulfur. Do not add fertilizer to the bed for two weeks after any such adjustment.

Which herbs will tolerate a soil that is more acidic than 6.0?

Dill, lemon verbena, lovage, pennyroyal, perilla, rue, scented geraniums, and thyme will grow well when the pH is 5.5. Angelica, basil, borage, calendula, catnip, lemon balm, rosemary, sage, sweet flag, and tansy will tolerate a pH as low as 5.0. Horehound, wintergreen, and yarrow will take a pH as low as 4.5. Sweet woodruff must be grown where the pH is 4.5 to 5.5.

Which herbs will tolerate an alkaline soil?

Basil, borage, burnet, calendula, caraway, chervil, coriander, cumin, fennel, horehound, horseradish, hyssop, lavender cotton, lemon balm, lovage, marjoram, mint, parsley, pennyroyal, rosemary, rue, sage, savory, sweet cicely, tarragon, watercress, and wormwood will grow in a pH up to 8.0. Lavender will grow in a pH up to 8.5. There are no herbs that will tolerate a pH higher than 8.5.

I have heard that there are different types of lime. Which is best for the garden?

If you use hydrated lime, which is quick acting, it should be applied several weeks prior to planting and watered in well to avoid any likelihood of its burning plants. Crushed limestone is much slower acting and longer lasting. Although it requires a heavier application, it can be used with less chance of burning. Dolomitic limestone is particularly good as it contains the essential trace element magnesium.

Planting and Nurturing the Seed Outdoors

I planned my herb garden on graph paper. What is the best way to transfer the design to the ground?

Using clothesline or lime, outline the design on the herb bed. The markings can be removed after the seeds have germinated or have been thinned.

Maggie Oster

Borage should be sown where it is to grow, as it is difficult to transplant.

Should the seedbed be wet or dry when I sow the seeds?

It is important to water the beds first to ensure that they are evenly moist before sowing. After sowing, water again. Seeds will not germinate unless they are in contact with moist soil.

How deep should I plant my seeds?

Instructions are usually given on seed packets, but a good rule of thumb is to plant them to a depth equal to their thickness.

I have trouble planting my seeds at the proper depth. Any ideas?

Make a furrow in the soil at the proper depth with the side of a trowel or a yardstick. After sowing, pinch the soil together with your fingers and firm it well to assure good contact between seeds and soil.

How close together should I plant my seeds?

Instructions will be given on the seed packet, but generally you should sow them twice as close together as the final recommended planting distance (see pages 132-33).

How often should I water my seedbeds?

The bed should never be allowed to dry out, so until the seeds germinate, water every day unless it rains. When seeds first germinate, they will continue to need daily watering. After a week, reduce the watering gradually until you are watering thoroughly just once a week. Deep watering encourages deep roots, and thus plants that will be better able to withstand heat and drought when summer comes.

What other care do I need to give my herb beds at this time?

Keep the beds well weeded, as weeds compete with herbs for light, water, and nutrients. Weeds also cause crowding and increased possibility of insects and disease. Remove weeds carefully so that the herbs are not disturbed, and water after weeding. Watch for signs of insects and disease. Slugs and snails, in particular, may damage young seedlings. Place bait after every watering or rain.

When should I thin my seedlings?

After seedlings are 2 to 3 inches high, or have developed two or three sets of true leaves, it is time to thin them.

What is the best way to thin seedlings?

On a cloudy day, if possible, water the ground first to make it easier to remove unwanted seedlings. Pull up the weakest before they crowd each other, leaving 2 to 6 inches between those remaining, according to their ultimate size. When those left begin to touch, again remove the weakest, leaving the remainder standing at the required distance apart. Pull seedlings carefully so the ones to remain are not disturbed. You can use the seedlings in another part of the garden, or share them with neighbors, friends, or family. Spread the operation over two to three weeks or as necessary as the plants develop.

What is meant by succession planting?

This entails planting seeds of an individual herb every one to two weeks, from spring planting time through early summer to midsummer, in order to have a continual supply of herbs. Succession planting is desirable for annual herbs that mature rapidly, especially when the entire plant is harvested by cutting it to the ground, or for herbs like dill and coriander that go to seed quickly in hot weather and stop producing foliage. In addition to dill and coriander, anise, chervil, and summer savory benefit most from succession planting, but it is an effective technique for any herb that is harvested continually or that matures quickly.

Which herb seeds should be sown where they are to grow because they are difficult to transplant?

Anise, borage, caraway, dill, fennel, horehound, lovage, parsley, perilla, safflower, savory, sesame, and sweet cicely.

OTHER FORMS OF HERB PROPAGATION

You may find it convenient to start herbs by methods other than seed. Cuttings taken from abundantly growing herbs allow you to carry young plants over the winter indoors; plants that are growing too densely can be divided; and new plants can be started from parent plants by a technique called layering.

Cuttings

Which herbs can I grow from stem cuttings?

Many herbs, especially perennials, can be grown from stem cuttings. These include anise hyssop, bee balm, Roman chamomile, costmary, germander, ginseng, horehound, hyssop, lavender, lemon balm, lemon verbena, marjoram, mint, oregano, pennyroyal, rosemary, rue, sage, scented geraniums, southernwood, sweet woodruff, tarragon, thyme, winter savory, and wormwood. Horseradish is increased by root cuttings.

What is the benefit of growing oregano, tarragon, and mint from cuttings?

True culinary (French) tarragon, as well as the artemisias, costmary, horseradish, lemon grass, and lemon verbena, cannot be grown from seeds and must be propagated by rooting cuttings or by division. Oregano and most mints are often not flavorful when grown from seeds, and cuttings are therefore better. Seeds sold as oregano may even sometimes be marjoram or savory seeds (see page 105). Another group of herbs, while they can be grown from seed, are often more successfully propagated from cuttings or division. These include English thyme (a named variety of common thyme), germander, ginseng, lavender, pennyroyal, rosemary, sage, scented geraniums, sweet woodruff, valerian, and winter savory.

When should cuttings be taken?

Because new growth does not root as successfully as established growth, cuttings should be taken after the new growth has become tougher, less tender and succulent. With most herbs, this will be in midsummer.

Can you please explain the correct procedure for taking and preparing a cutting?

Make the cut just above a leaf. Carefully remove the bottom two to three leaves to expose the leaf nodes, which are the points where the new roots will grow. If there are any flowers or flower buds on the cutting, they must be removed. Most perennial herbs root easily and need no rooting hormone. Ginseng and other woody perennials benefit from dipping the end of the cutting in a hormone such as Rootone.

How long should cuttings be?

That depends to some extent on the plant. A cutting should have about four to six leaves above the cut.

What type of medium should I use to root cuttings?

Use the same medium as for sowing seeds, which is half peat moss and half perlite, vermiculite, or coarse sand. Cuttings may also be rooted in clean, sharp sand—a coarser sand than beach sand, which is available at building supply stores and garden centers.

How deeply should the cutting be planted in the medium?

Fill the container to within ¼ inch of the top with moist medium. Make a hole with a dibble (a small tool used for making planting holes) or a pencil, and insert the cutting so that the leaf nodes you have exposed are completely covered with medium. Press the medium gently around the cutting.

Why do my cuttings wilt when I first place them in rooting medium?

Cuttings wilt because they have lost moisture and do not have roots yet to replenish the lost moisture. To ease this problem, place the container with the cuttings inside a clear plastic bag, or

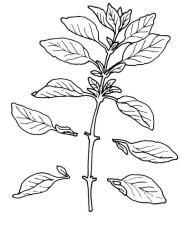

To take cuttings, cut just above a leaf, remove lower leaves on cutting, to expose leaf nodes.

place a large glass jar over the container and the cuttings. When roots have developed, the bag or jar may be removed.

How can I tell when cuttings are rooted?

After about three weeks, gently tug on a leaf. If the cutting has rooted, it will offer resistance. If it can be removed from the medium easily, return it to the container and test it again in several more weeks.

In what type of light should cuttings be placed while they are rooting?

Indoors, keep cuttings in bright light, but not full sun, until they have rooted. Then move them into full sun.

Can I root cuttings outdoors?

Yes, cuttings can be rooted outdoors during the summer. Place them either in containers or in well-prepared soil, in a spot in partial shade, and cover them with plastic or a glass jar just as for indoor cuttings. Start them early enough so that they will be rooted at least six weeks before the first fall frost. Cuttings can be rooted late in the season in a cold frame.

I forgot to take cuttings during the summer. Is it too late to do it in the fall?

If you don't have a cold frame and expect frost soon, take cuttings and root them indoors. Transplant them outside early the next spring.

Division

Which herbs are usually increased by division?

Most perennial herbs, except those that have deep tap roots, can be divided. These include angelica, anise hyssop, bee balm, catnip, chives, costmary, germander, horehound, hyssop, lavender cotton, lemon balm, lemon grass, lovage, mint, oregano, pennyroyal, rosemary, rue, sage, sweet woodruff, tansy, tarragon, thyme, valerian, watercress, winter savory, wormwood, and yarrow.

When is the best time to divide herbs?

Herbs may be divided either in early to mid-spring when growth starts, or in early fall about six weeks before the first fall frost.

How are herbs divided?

Carefully dig up the plant, damaging as little of the root system as possible. If necessary, wash soil from the roots so you

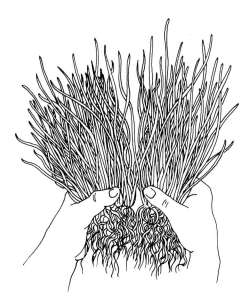

Many herbs can be divided by gently pulling them apart with your fingers.

can better see what you're doing. Carefully pull the roots apart with your fingers. If they are too strong to pull apart by hand, use a trowel or knife to divide them. Replant before the roots dry out.

Should I cut the tops back after I divide herbs?

If you divide in early spring when top growth is small, it will not be necessary to cut the tops back. If you divide herbs in the fall, cut the tops back by about a half when dividing.

What care should I give plants after they are divided?

Treat them as you would a new seedling. Water the soil right after the plants are transplanted, and again daily for about a week. After that, water as necessary. If the tops wilt, resume watering or place plastic or a glass jar over the divisions until they are no longer wilting and have started to grow.

I would like to get a half dozen or so mint plants to give away to friends. Do I have to dig up my whole clump of mint?

No. You can simply dig into the clump with a sharp shovel and chop out pieces for re-planting. Rugged plants, such as mint or horseradish, can be handled quite roughly and still survive and spread.

Layering

What does layering plants mean?

This is a method of propagation that is accomplished by taking a long, flexible stem of a perennial (or other woody plant) and securing it to, or slightly under, the ground. Sometimes a slight cut is made at the point where the stem touches the ground. Where the stem contacts the ground, it will root, and in time can be cut from the mother plant and transplanted.

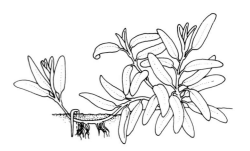

To layer perennial herbs, fasten down a long, flexible stem using a large hairpin.

How should I secure the plant to the ground?

You can weight it down with a rock, or pin it down with a piece of metal, such as a large hairpin.

When should I layer my plants?

Plants are layered during the summer and will usually be rooted by fall. If roots are still small, wait until the following spring to move the new plant.

Which plants in my herb garden can I layer?

The plants most commonly layered are lavender, lavender cotton, rosemary, sage, thyme, and winter savory.

PURCHASED SEEDLINGS
— • —

When should I go shopping for my herb plants?

Purchase plants as close to the time that you are going to plant them as possible. If you buy them too early, you will have to water them every day to keep them from drying out, or you may even be faced with the possibility of a late frost.

What should I look for when buying plants?

Look for healthy, dark green plants that show no sign of insects or disease, are not too tall or spindly, and show signs of new growth. If you are buying herbs whose leaves you will be using in cooking, smell them or take a tiny taste of a leaf to make sure you like the flavor.

I ordered herbs from a mail-order firm, and when they arrived, they were dried out. What should I do?

Water the plants right away and keep them in a cool area out of direct sun until they revive. Then plant them. If they do not make it, write to the company and ask for a replacement.

TRANSPLANTING INTO THE GARDEN
— • —

Whether you begin your own herb plants by seed or other methods of propagation, or purchase plants at a reliable nursery, the techniques for getting them off to a healthy start in the ground outdoors are the same.

When should seedlings that were raised in flats be transplanted? How many times?

The first transplanting should be done indoors when the seedlings form their first true leaves (see page 25). Many plants, when they are 2 or 3 inches high, benefit from a second transplant to individual pots before they are moved outdoors. However, seedlings grown in flats can be thinned and the remaining plants allowed to grow in the original tray or flat until they are ready to go outdoors. They may need a light feeding before being set in the garden. Move plants to the garden according to their hardiness. Plant hardy annuals, perennials, and biennials in the garden any time after the soil can be worked in mid-spring; transplant tender herbs when all danger of frost has passed.

Is there anything I need to do to get my herbs ready to be moved into the garden?

Yes. They must be put through a process called *hardening off*. One week before you transplant them into the garden, move the plants outdoors and place them in a shady spot. Bring them back inside at night. Each day, move them into greater light, and toward the end of the week, leave the plants out all night.

How can I remove small plants from their containers at transplanting time without damaging the roots?

Most purchased plants today are grown in individual cells or pots. Removal is easy; if the plants don't fall out easily, they can be pushed up from the bottom. Water thoroughly a few hours before transplanting.

If your plants are not in individual cells, with an old knife or a small mason's trowel, cut the soil into squares, each with a plant in the center. This should leave the plant root systems almost intact.

Herbs that have been grown individually in peat pots need not be removed from their pots when they are planted. It is advisable, however, to break or peel the pot in a few places to help the roots penetrate into the soil more readily. Be sure to set the top edge of the pot *below* the soil level, or it will act as a wick or sponge, drawing water from the soil. Because the water then quickly evaporates, instead of nourishing the plant, the plant can suffer. Water thoroughly after planting and as necessary thereafter until the plant roots have penetrated through the pot into the soil and the plant has started to grow.

Peat pots should be broken somewhat before planting, and rims should be set below soil level.

What is the right technique for setting out (planting) herb plants?

Water both the ground and the transplants first. Remove the plants from the flats or the pots with as little root disturbance as possible. Stab the trowel in the soil, pull toward you, set the plant in the hole, remove the trowel, push the soil around the roots, press the soil firmly, and leave a slight depression around the stem to trap water.

How far apart should I space herbs when thinning them or planting them out?

The distance varies according to the type of herb and its habit of growth. A rough rule is a distance equal to one half of its mature height. Look for directions on the seed packet or plant label, or follow the guidelines for individual herbs in Chapter 5.

What is the best time of day to transplant?

Move plants late in the afternoon, or on a cloudy day, to help reduce transplanting shock.

How should I care for my transplants?

Water them well after transplanting and again daily for about a week until the transplants are well established and show signs of growth. Gradually reduce watering until about once per week, which should be sufficient for the remainder of the summer unless it becomes quite hot and dry. Keep the beds well weeded and watch for signs of insects and diseases, especially slugs and snails (see pages 49-55). Some transplants may wilt at first, but daily misting and/or shading will help them to revive quickly.

After I transplanted my basil seedlings, we had an unexpected late frost, and I lost them all. Is there anything I could have done?

Yes. Basil is particularly susceptible to frost, but other tender herbs can be damaged by frost as well. If frost is predicted, place hot caps or styrofoam cups over the seedlings in the evening, and remove them in the morning. Watering the seedlings can also help, since when the water on the leaves freezes, the layer of ice insulates the plant cells and keeps them from freezing.

Use hot caps to protect tender herbs from late spring and early fall frosts.

NURTURING HERBS IN THEIR PERMANENT BEDS

How often should I water my herb garden?

Under normal circumstances, herbs should receive a thorough (1 inch) watering once a week. If it becomes very hot during the summer, or if your garden is in a windy spot, or if your soil is very sandy, it may need watering more often. Overwatering an herb garden causes most plants to lose their flavor or fragrance—or it may even kill the plants.

How can I determine that my soil is receiving 1 inch of water?

To check the amount that you are watering, place an empty coffee can halfway between the sprinkler and the farthest point it reaches. Time how long it takes for 1 inch of water to accumulate in the can. Presuming the water pressure remains constant, run your sprinklers for the amount of time it took for 1 inch of water to collect in the can. You can also place a rain gauge in the herb bed to measure the amount of water.

Why do I need to water my herb garden only once a week? Couldn't I sprinkle it lightly every day?

This is the worst thing you could do. Light, frequent watering encourages shallow roots; then if it becomes hot or if you go away for a few days, the herbs will not be able to survive as well. Deep watering encourages the roots to grow down. Some herbs must have dry soil, and watering daily would kill them (see page 33).

Is it a good idea to water my herb garden with an overhead sprinkler? If not, what other method could I use?

Overhead watering is perfectly acceptable in many instances, and actually cools the plants and washes dirt off the foliage. Where leaf spot or mildew disease is a problem, water in the morning so the foliage is not wet during the night. You could also use soaker hoses to alleviate this problem, as well as to avoid damaging tall or weak-stemmed plants with overhead watering.

Because we get very little rain in the summer, we have watering restrictions. Can I still have an herb garden?

Many herbs actually like dry soil. For those herbs that prefer moist soil, mix a quantity of organic matter into the soil when preparing beds and mulch with additional organic matter, which will retain water.

Which herbs should be pinched back and at what stage?

To keep them compact and bushy, plants of angelica, basil, borage, geraniums, mint, pennyroyal, and perilla should be pinched back (see page 27) when they are 2 to 4 inches high. Herbs that are not being grown for their flowers or seed can be cut back during midsummer if they get too tall or spindly.

Why is the recommendation given to remove the flowers of some herbs before they develop?

The leaves of herbs grown for their foliage, such as basil, are generally more flavorful or more highly scented before flowers form. Also, because many plants stop growing once flowers form, you will receive a more abundant harvest of leaves if you remove flowers.

Should herbs that are grown for their flowers be treated in any special way?

Removing flowers as soon as they are ready for harvest will encourage more flowers to form.

I never grew herbs because I had heard that so many of them needed staking. Is this true?

A few, such as angelica, anise, and valerian, need to be staked. Bee balm and dill also tend to flop over, but if they are grown close together, they will prop each other up. In addition, look for shorter varieties of dill that do not need staking.

What type of material can I use as a stake?

Try bamboo sticks, metal poles, or most anything that will hold the plants up. With a twist tie or a string, tie the plants loosely to the stakes so that the stems will not be pinched or damaged. For large plants, set two to four stakes around the plant and tie string in a circle around the stakes and the plant. Large herbs can also be grown in wire tomato or peony cages.

Can I clip the plants in my knot garden at any time during the summer?

Clip plants as needed to keep them neat and trim. Woody plants such as lavender cotton, lavender, and germander should not be clipped after midsummer. A late pruning would force out new growth that would not harden off (see page 38) before freezing temperatures.

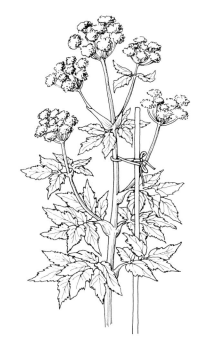

Make a figure eight tie when staking tall, heavy herbs.

Isn't it true that some herbs can spread throughout my garden and choke out other plants?

Yes. Plants that do this are said by gardeners to be "invasive." Some of the worst culprits among herbs are angelica, bee balm, burnet, catnip, chamomile, chervil, costmary, dill, horseradish, mint, pennyroyal, tansy, white yarrow, and wormwood.

Other than to avoid growing those herbs that become invasive, what can I do to control this problem?

Some herbs are invasive because they drop seeds (see the next question). For these herbs, do not allow flowers to form, or cut the flowers off before they drop seeds to the ground. Others are invasive because of a vigorous root system. These can be kept in control by inserting metal or plastic edging down into the ground at the border of the herb beds or around the individual plants. Such plants can also be grown in cinder blocks, PVC drainage pipe, or containers plunged into the ground to keep them in bounds. Horseradish grows freely from pieces of the roots that remain in the ground after harvesting. This is difficult to control, so delegate a section of the garden for horseradish only.

Insert metal or plastic edging down into the ground to control such herbs as bee balm, the roots of which spread rapidly.

I have noticed that plants of angelica, anise hyssop, burnet, chamomile, chervil, dill, and lemon balm come up each year. Are these plants perennials?

Some are, and some are not. If the plants are small, what you are seeing are seedlings that grew from seeds that dropped the previous season.

Can I leave the self-sown seedlings growing in the garden, or should I pull them up?

You can leave them as long as they don't make the planting overcrowded. You will probably need to thin some of them out. In a formal garden, you will want to remove all of them or they will upset the balance and symmetry. If self-sown "volunteers" become a nuisance, be sure to remove all flowers before seeds form and drop.

Can I save seeds from my herb plants for use next year?

Most herbs are not hybrids, therefore seeds can be saved and grown the following year and come true to type. Seeds of angelica, anise, lovage, and valerian must be sown right after they are harvested or they will not germinate. Seeds of mint and oregano may produce plants that have little flavor.

Is weeding really that important?

We wish we could say no, but actually weeds harbor insects and disease, and compete with the herbs for light, water, and nutrients.

Do you have any suggestions to lighten the chore of weeding?

Since many weeds are spread by seeds, it is important to pull weeds before they flower and the seeds fall and sprout. There are several methods of keeping weeds down. Besides hand-pulling, you can weed mature plantings with a hoe, and keep plants well mulched.

Can I apply liquid weedkiller to the herbs in my garden?

This would be unwise, for it would probably do as much harm to the herbs as to the weeds. Weedkiller might also be unsafe for use near plants that are raised for culinary purposes.

I have read about using black plastic as a mulch. Does this prevent weeds?

Yes, it does, and quite well. Be sure to punch holes in the plastic, though, so water can penetrate to the plants' roots. If you don't like the appearance of black plastic, cover it with a mulch of leaf mold, bark chips, pine needles, or other attractive material.

What are the other advantages of mulch in addition to controlling weeds?

Mulch keeps the soil cool and moist, reducing the need for watering. It also adds a decorative finish to the herb garden.

What materials make good mulches?

Use an organic material, such as shredded leaves, bark chips, pine needles (unless the herbs require alkaline soils; see pages 31-32), or hulls of some kind. Each spring, unless you are growing herbs that do better without added organic matter, mix the mulch in with the soil to enrich it, and add new mulch.

Can I use grass clippings as mulch?

Yes, provided you dry them first, and there are no weed seeds in the grass. As they decompose, grass clippings give off a great deal of heat, which could damage the roots of herbs.

Will I need to provide winter mulch to my perennial herbs?

That depends on where you live and how hardy your herbs are. If you live near the edge of an herb's hardiness zone (see pages 2 and 134), winter protection will be helpful.

What should I use for winter protection?

Try oak leaves, pine needles (although these will make the soil more acidic), evergreen boughs, soil, or even shredded newspaper.

Heavy mulching is one of the best ways to prevent the spread of weeds.

When should winter protection be applied?

To allow the base of the plants to harden off sufficiently, put protection on *after* the ground has frozen. Placing winter protection on too early will also encourage rodents to make their winter homes there.

I have had problems keeping lavender alive over the winter in my Ohio garden. I protect it, but it usually dies. What should I do?

Check to be certain that the lavender you are growing is winter hardy; several varieties of lavender will not survive the cold winters of the north. Lavender, as well as tarragon, sage, and thyme, is damaged more by wet soil and poor drainage over the winter than it is by cold. Make sure your soil has excellent drainage. Do not place these plants in low areas of the garden where water may collect. Where severe problems exist, place a small wooden or rigid foam box over the plants to keep rain and snow off them during the winter.

When should winter protection be removed?

Remove it gradually in the spring as soon as plants start growing.

CONTAINER-GROWN HERBS

Which herbs can I plant into containers on my patio?

Almost any low-growing herb will grow well in a container. Select one that is in proportion to the container. Try basil, calendula, chamomile, chives, lavender, lavender cotton, parsley, sage, scented geraniums, or thyme, among others.

What type of soil should I use in containers? Is it all right to dig soil from the garden?

No, garden soil by itself should not be used. Root growth will not be good because the soil is too heavy, and, in addition, it can introduce insects and diseases. For most herbs, use a soilless mix of peat moss with perlite and/or vermiculite. Those that like infertile soil can be grown in garden soil combined with a small amount of soilless mix to lighten it.

Can I grow herbs in a large ceramic urn?

So that roots don't become waterlogged, containers should have drainage holes. If your urn does not have them and you don't want to punch holes in the bottom, add a thick layer of gravel to the bottom.

How often should my containers be watered?

That depends on the size of the container and the moisture requirements of the herb you are growing. If you are growing an

Maggie Oster

An awkward corner can be made more interesting by an attractive arrangement of container-grown herbs.

herb that likes dry soil, allow the top inch of the container to dry out before watering. If you are growing an herb that likes average to moist growing conditions, water the container as soon as the medium starts to dry out. Small containers will naturally need to be watered more often than large ones. Check every day to be sure; when it is very hot or if it is windy, you may need to water daily or even twice a day. It will be convenient to have a water source nearby if you have a large number of containers.

How should I fertilize container-grown herbs?

Because containers are watered more frequently, the fertilizer washes out through the soil very quickly. Therefore, feed lightly but more often than you would fertilize the same herbs in the ground. Too much fertilizer usually does more harm than good when growing herbs.

Last year the herbs in my containers did not grow evenly. What should I do to get even growth this summer?

They probably were growing towards the light. Rotate containers regularly so this does not happen. If the container is large and heavy, place it on a dolly so it can be turned more easily.

Place large pots on dollies so that they can be moved more easily.

Can I leave my potted herbs out on the terrace in New York during the winter?

No, they will not survive. If possible, replant perennial or biennial herbs in open ground for the winter, or dig a hole and place the entire pot in the ground until spring.

Can I bring my containers inside for the winter?

Yes, if they are small enough, if the herb is a type that will grow well indoors, and if you have a room with enough sun or can provide plant lights. Otherwise, take cuttings and start new plants, and then replant the containers next spring.

Which herbs will do well if I move them inside?

If grown outdoors all summer in pots, not in the ground, basil, chives, scented geraniums, lemon verbena, marjoram, parsley, thyme, summer savory, and rosemary may be brought indoors for the winter. Either move the potted plants indoors, or start new plants from seed, division, or cuttings (see pages 17-37).

Container-grown herbs can be placed near the doorway for last-minute additions to summer meals.

Derek Fell

How should I care for mature herbs indoors?

Herbs should be grown indoors on a sunny windowsill or under fluorescent lights. Water them when the top of the soil surface has dried out. Most will be happy at normal room temperature, except rosemary, which likes a cool (55° F.) room. Do not fertilize from mid-fall through mid-spring. At other times, feed lightly.

If I grow herbs indoors under fluorescent lights, how many hours each day should the lights be on?

Keep the lights on for fourteen to sixteen hours each day. Plants should be about 12 to 18 inches below the lights.

I've tried to grow herbs indoors during the winter, but they don't do well. The leaves yellow and dry out.

Perhaps the humidity is too low. Grow the herbs on pebble trays that can be kept filled with water; run a humidifier in the room; or put a bowl of water or a wet towel on the heat source. As the water evaporates, the moisture in the air will increase.

3 *Herb Problems and How to Solve Them*

One of the nicest things about herb gardening is that herbs are seldom troubled by diseases or insect pests. In fact, many herbs make excellent companion plants to *repel* harmful insects in vegetable and flower gardens. For example, chives, peppermint, and tansy are said to repel aphids; basil, the asparagus beetle; catnip and tansy, the Japanese beetle; coriander, the spider mite; thyme and wormwood, the whitefly. Some herbs, such as wormwood, pennyroyal, sage, and tansy, can serve as the basis of repellent sprays against insect pests, and pennyroyal is thought to repel mosquitos. Hung in closets or laid in drawers, lavender and wormwood are old, and effective, guards against moths.

If herbs—particularly those raised indoors, which may be more susceptible to attack by the common pests of houseplants—are bothered by insects, try using nonchemical control, rotenone, or pyrethrum. (See Herbs, as repellents, in the Index.) If all else fails and you feel you must resort to chemical control, be sure to use products formulated for vegetables, and follow carefully the label instructions regarding the waiting period before harvest and consumption.

What are the tiny green, semi-transparent insects that appear along stems and flower buds? The plants are distorted and withered and the leaves have curled. There is also a black, sooty substance on the leaves.

Aphids, or plant lice, may be green, as you describe, as well as yellow, brown, black, or red. Not only do they suck juices from

INSECT PESTS

◀ *Most herbs are remarkably free of pest and disease problems, particularly if good cultural practices are followed.*

49

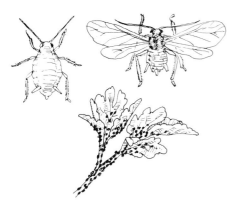

Aphid. These insects spread disease from plant to plant as they suck juices from stems, leaves, buds, and flowers.

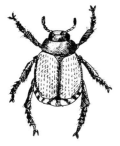

Japanese beetle. These common garden pests can be controlled biologically with milky spore disease.

Spider mite. Mites are especially prevalent during very hot, dry weather.

plants, but they also can carry many diseases. Wash them off with a stream of water, use insecticidal soap, or spray with rotenone or pyrethrum.

Which herbs are most likely to be bothered by aphids?

Aphids can be troublesome to a large number of herbs, but those most severely affected are angelica, calendula, caraway, costmary, cumin, dill, horseradish, mint, parsley, tansy, valerian, wormwood, and yarrow.

What is the black sooty substance that appears on the leaves of herbs when aphids are present?

Aphids secrete a sticky substance called honeydew, on which black, powdery mold often grows. This can be washed off with water after the aphids are controlled.

Holes are being chewed in the leaves and flowers of some of my herbs, probably by the small, hard-shelled insects on the plants. What do you suggest?

There are a number of beetles that attack herbs, although they are not usually a serious problem in the herb garden. If they are few in number, hand-pick them off. Traps sometimes work, but can often attract beetles from a neighbor's garden as well. If the infestation is severe, release beneficial nematodes (available through suppliers of beneficial insects; see Appendix). Use milky spore disease (*Bacillus popilliae*) to control Japanese beetles.

Which herbs are most likely to be attacked by beetles?

Borage, calendula, horseradish, mint, and wormwood are their favorite host plants.

The leaves of my herbs have turned a dull color, with black specks on their undersides and webbing between them. What can I do?

You have spider mites, and if you can see webbing, the infestation is very advanced. Mites do not like water, so keep the plants well watered, and syringe the undersides of the leaves with clear water. Try spraying with pyrethrum. If the problem continues, it may be best to remove the plant and dispose of it, rather than risk the pests spreading to other plants.

Mites were more of a problem last summer than they had been in the past. Why was this?

Perhaps it was hotter and drier than usual. Mites are most prevalent under these conditions. When it is very hot and dry, spray the undersides of the leaves with water every day to help prevent mite infestations.

I have a heavy infestation of mites on my mint plants this summer. Will they spread to other plants?

They may. Mites like scented geraniums, lemon verbena, parsley, valerian, and wormwood, in particular.

How can I control the plant bugs I see on my lavender plants?

These small sucking insects are hard to control. They are very active, produce several generations of new insects a season, and occur on many kinds of plants, stinging the flower buds and spotting the leaves. Dust or spray with rotenone. Clean up all trash and weeds to remove the bug's favorite places for hibernation.

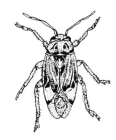

Plant bug. A small, sucking insect, the plant bug is sometimes hard to control.

Will the plant bug infest plants other than lavender in my herb garden?

In addition to lavender, plant bugs like calendula, mint, and valerian.

When I brush against the valerian in the garden, a cloud of tiny white insects appears. Are they doing damage?

Yes. These are whiteflies, which suck juices from the plants. They can be controlled with insecticidal soap, pyrethrum, or commercially available, sticky, yellow traps, the color of which attracts them.

Groups of whiteflies are often well hidden on the underside of such leaves as this mint.

Ron West

Some of my plants wilted and lost their color. When I dug them up, I noticed swellings on the roots. Is this related to their demise?

Yes, this was most likely nematode damage, but you'd have to have your soil tested to be sure. Minimize risk by not planting the same kind of plant in the same space for three to four years. Plant the marigolds *Tagetes erecta* or *T. patula* in affected spots to kill the nematodes. These insects can be serious pests in the herb garden, their favorite plants being basil, caraway, chamomile, coriander, fennel, ginseng, horehound, horseradish, hyssop, mint, parsley, sage, and tansy.

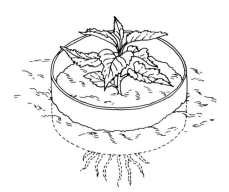

Place a 2-inch wide cardboard collar around herb stems to protect against cutworm damage.

After I planted my young herb seedlings in the garden, something ate them at night. What might it have been?

If the plants were cut off at the soil surface and left lying on the ground, cutworms were at work. Prevent them from doing damage by inserting a plastic or cardboard collar around the stems when you plant them. If the foliage was eaten and you see silvery streaks nearby, slugs or snails are present. Trap these in shallow saucers of stale beer.

What can one do to get rid of the soft, white, fungus scale on mint? Scraping it off doesn't do much good.

Neither a fungus nor a scale, mealybugs are your culprits. These soft, white, sucking insects resemble tiny balls of cotton. Mealybugs, like most sucking insects, thrive in a dry atmosphere, but too little water cannot "cause" them. Also, if the plants are unhealthy from a waterlogged soil, they may succumb more readily to mealybug injury. Wash, or if possible actually scrub, the plant with insecticidal soap. Individual adults can be killed by swabbing them with rubbing alcohol.

Slug. Chewed foliage and evidence of silvery streaks suggest the presence of slugs and snails.

What other herbs are likely to be bothered by mealybugs?

Mealybugs attack calendula, thyme, valerian, and wormwood as well as mint.

Mealybug. If you see soft, fuzzy, white spots on the underside of leaves, you may have an infestation of mealybugs.

How can I control the caterpillars that appear in the garden in spring?

If experience has shown caterpillars to be a problem in the past, spray in advance of an infestation with the biological control *Bacillus thuringiensis*, commonly called Bt.

Are all plants susceptible to caterpillars?

No, those most likely to be bothered are calendula, caraway, dill, horseradish, lavender, and parsley. Plants that are situated near trees may be attacked more than those that are not.

My hyssop plants are covered with small, oval, hard, crusty growths. What are these?

These are scale insects, which suck the plant juices from the stems and eventually weaken and kill the plants. Wash the plant with insecticidal soap.

I sowed herb seeds this spring. The seedlings germinated and started to grow, then suddenly fell over and died. What did I do wrong?

This sounds like damping-off fungus, which can be lethal to seedlings. Use only sterile medium that has not been used before. Do not overwater, and provide good air circulation.

Some of my herbs lost their color and stopped growing, and I removed them from the ground. The roots were dark in color and appeared slimy. What caused this?

The plants had root rot, which can be caused by a number of fungi. Avoid this problem by providing good drainage and by not overwatering your herb garden.

Which herbs are most susceptible to root rot?

Root rot can theoretically occur anytime the ground has poor drainage and is constantly wet. However, the most susceptible herbs are angelica, anise, catnip, chamomile, dill, fennel, ginseng, horseradish, lavender, parsley, rosemary, safflower, sage, thyme, and valerian.

Spots have developed on the foliage of some of my herbs. What should I do?

Leaf spot disease is best treated by removing the spotted leaves from the plant and the ground. Water plants only in the morning, and, if possible, do not let the foliage get wet.

On what herbs might leaf spot disease occur?

Leaf spot disease attacks a number of herbs, including angelica, anise, bee balm, borage, burnet, catnip, cumin, dill, ginseng, horehound, horseradish, lavender, lemon balm, lemon grass, mint, parsley, pennyroyal, sesame, and tansy.

What is the white powder that develops on foliage in early fall?

Powdery mildew is a fungus disease that is most prevalent when days are warm and nights are cool. Cut off infected plant parts and water only in the morning. If possible, do not water from overhead. Improve air circulation by not crowding plants.

HERB PLANT DISEASES

—— • ——

Which herbs are most likely to be affected by mildew?

Mildew is not a serious problem for herbs, but may be seen on burnet, horseradish, mint, pennyroyal, safflower, sage, tansy, and wormwood.

Leaves of my mint plants have developed an orange powder on the undersides. What is this?

This is rust, a fungus disease. Remove and destroy all infected leaves, and water only in the morning.

I never had rust in my Pennsylvania garden, but I have moved to Oregon where it often occurs. What might be the problem?

Rust is a particular problem in the Pacific Northwest because it occurs most frequently when the weather is cool and damp.

Is rust a problem only on mint?

Rust is more serious on mint than on other herbs, but it also affects angelica, anise, bee balm, burnet, chives, ginseng, sage, tansy, and valerian.

There is a grayish brown powder on the flowers and flower buds of my scented geraniums. How can I get rid of this?

Botrytis blight usually occurs when it is cool or cloudy. Cut off infected plant parts. Do not overwater. It is primarily a problem of scented geraniums but may also affect catnip, lemon balm, and thyme.

After reaching full growth and flowering size, my caraway dried up and died. What was the cause?

It may have been aster yellows, a virus disease transmitted from diseased to healthy plants by leafhoppers. When the plant loses its chlorophyll, the leaves turn yellow and the blossoms turn green. Plants are usually stunted and will eventually die.

About a third of my scented geranium cuttings have shrivelled at the ground, turned black, and died. What is the cause?

Either a fungal or a bacterial stem rot. Take cuttings from healthy plants and place them in clean, fresh sand or a mixture of peat moss and perlite that has not been used before. Keep them on the dry side, as the disease is most prevalent when the medium is overwatered. Drainage must be excellent.

My scented geraniums have leaves with small, water-soaked blisters. What should I do about this?

They suffer from oedema, a common problem of all geraniums. Once infected, the plant can't be cured, but good cultural practices such as providing excellent drainage and taking care not to overwater will prevent this disease.

Will other herbs be affected by aster yellows?

Yes, chamomile, dill, parsley, and sage are also prone to aster yellows.

How can I prevent aster yellows?

Only by getting rid of the insects, often leafhoppers, that transmit the disease. Remove affected plants immediately, so there will be no source of infection. Spray frequently with pyrethrum to kill the leafhoppers.

Last year the leaves of my safflower plants developed small holes in them and the plant became weakened. Is this an insect problem? I saw no signs of insects.

It could be an insect, but it is likely that it is spot anthracnose, a fungus disease. As small areas of leaf tissue die, they lose their color and fall out of the leaf, leaving small spots behind. Remove infected leaves and don't let the plants become overcrowded.

4 Enjoying the Herb Garden

Both fresh and dried herbs are perfect no-salt seasonings for all kinds of dishes, from appetizers right through desserts, as well as for butters, vinegars, jellies, and teas. Whether you choose classic combinations, such as a sauce seasoned with *fines herbes*, or enjoy a non-traditional experiment featuring fennel and fish, or tomatoes and tarragon, herbs will enliven your cooking and give pleasure to those you cook for. Equally satisfying are the non-culinary uses of herbs, particularly for dried flower arrangements and scented soaps and potpourri. A few simple principles followed at harvest will ensure maximum success.

When can I harvest leaves for fresh use?

The leaves of most culinary herbs have enough flavor throughout the season that you can harvest them at any time. Pick healthy, green leaves as you need them, being careful not to injure the stem when you remove the leaves. If plants are small, do not remove too many leaves from one stem.

My plants have become a good size by midsummer. Can I cut them back and use the leaves?

Yes, and not only will you enjoy the harvest but you will encourage the plant to become bushier. You can either cut them back with hedge shears or pinch out the growing tips.

◀ *Artemisia, lavender, tansy, and a variety of other herbs and flowers decorate this handsome wreath.*

HARVESTING
AND STORING HERB
LEAVES AND SEEDS
•

What do I need to do to leaves before using them fresh?

Nothing, except to wash and dry them quickly by blotting them with a paper towel.

When should I cut leaves for drying?

Most herbs are at the height of their flavor when the flowers are just starting to bloom.

Are there exceptions to this rule?

A few. Read the individual descriptions in Chapter 5 to be sure. Lavender contains the most fragrant oil just before the flowers open, and sage, too, should be picked as soon as flower buds appear. Hyssop is best when its flowers are in full bloom. Thyme and sage, on the other hand, are flavorful throughout the season.

Does it matter what time of day I cut herbs?

Yes, cut them on a dry, sunny morning after the dew has dried, but before the sun is hot.

How far back should I cut the stems to harvest leaves for drying?

That depends on the time of year and whether the plants are annuals or perennials. Established perennial plants such as oregano, thyme, mint, and sage can usually be harvested two or three times during the summer if you cut just one-third of their height. The last harvest should be light and completed in early fall. Annual herbs may be cut to the ground in the fall.

What is the best way to dry herb leaves?

There are two basic methods of drying herbs: drying them on screens, or hanging them upside down (see questions following). Check the individual plant entries in Chapter 5 to see which method is best for the herb you are growing. Both methods require a dry spot with good air circulation so that the air will absorb the moisture without destroying the flavorful oils. Herb leaves should also be dried in the dark, or at least out of direct sunlight.

I'd like to hang my herbs to dry them. Could you describe the proper procedure?

Cut the stems as long as possible and pick off any yellow, damaged, or dead foliage. Wash the herbs in cool water, and blot them dry with a paper towel. Tie the ends together in small bunches of about a dozen stems and hang the herbs upside down from the ceiling, rafters, or from an old-fashioned clothes-drying rack. Choose a place out of direct light, with good air circulation. After a week or two, they should be dry and crisp. Remove the leaves carefully and store them in an airtight container.

Cut long stems and tie bundles of about a dozen together to hang upside down in an airy place until dry and crisp.

Fifteen Popular Herbs and Their Usage

HERB	INTERPLANT IDEAS	CULINARY SUGGESTIONS	GIFTS
Angelica		Natural sweetener for tart fruits; candied stems	Fancy pastries decorated with candied stems
Basil	Companion to tomatoes; dislikes rue	Tomatoes and tomato dishes, minestrone soup, pesto sauce for pasta, eggs, fish, lamb, zucchini casseroles	Pesto sauce in decorative jars, purple basil vinegar, container-grown basil, dried herb
Catnip	Deters flea beetles		Handmade catnip toys, fresh cuttings, tea leaves
Chives	Companion to carrots	Omelettes, cold soups, green salads, cheese, fish, dips, vegetable dishes	Fresh cream cheese and chive spread, container-grown chives
Dill	Companion to *Brassicas*; dislikes carrots	Leaves: cucumbers, salads, fish (especially salmon), potatoes, vegetables, sour cream and yogurt, egg dishes. Seeds: pickles, salad dressings, meats, breads	Jars of homemade dill pickles, dill vinegar, fresh dill weed
Fennel	Plant alone	Salmon and oily fish, salad dressings, breads and rolls, apple pie	Freshly baked seeded rolls and breads, fennel-flavored oil
Marjoram	Throughout garden	Poultry seasoning, meats and game, sauces and marinades, soups, egg dishes	Bouquet garni, sachets, tea, herb butter
Mint	Companion to cabbage and tomatoes	Summertime beverages, cold soups (especially fruit soups), fruits, minted peas, salads, lamb, teas, candies	Mint jelly, mint tea, candies, sachets, root divisions
Oregano	Throughout garden	Pizza, pasta, Mexican and Italian dishes, tomatoes and tomato dishes, soups, eggs, ground beef, vegetable casseroles	Dried Italian seasoning mix, container-grown plant, flavored oil
Parsley	Tomatoes	Soups, stews, salads, all vegetables, fish, steaks, garnish	Bouquet garni, tea, fresh sprigs, container-grown plant
Rosemary	Sage, beans, broccoli, cabbage, carrots	Meats (especially lamb and pork), poultry, game, marinades and sauces, carrots, breads	Meat marinade mix, sachet, tea, hair rinse, container-grown plant
Sage	Rosemary, carrots, cabbage; dislikes cucumber	Poultry stuffing, pork, cheeses, breads	Sage cheese, stuffing mix, tea, hair rinse
Savory	Beans, onions	All bean dishes, stuffings, fish, soups, vegetable dishes and juices	Bouquet garni, tea, container-grown herb, sachets
Tarragon	Throughout garden	Sauce béarnaise, fish, chicken, eggs, cold summer salads, salad dressings, vinegar, soups, vegetable juices	Flavored vinegar, tarragon jelly, fines herbes mix
Thyme	Cabbage	Meat, chicken, fish, soups and stocks, stews, vegetables, sauces, salads, clam chowder, poultry stuffing	Bouquet garni, tea, sachets, cuttings

Positive Images, Jerry Howard

Herbs may be dried and stored in a cool, dark place, waiting for use in the kitchen or in potpourris or winter decorations.

I have heard that herbs being dried should have a paper bag placed over them. Why is this necessary (other than to collect seed)?

The paper bag is not necessary, but it does have advantages. Herbs retain more flavor when dried in the dark, and the bag will also keep dust off the leaves and catch any leaves that drop.

Which herbs should be dried upside down?

This method will work well with most herbs, providing the stems are long enough. Marjoram, mint, rosemary, sage, savory, and thyme are often dried this way. If the stems are short or you are drying individual leaves, drying on a screen is the only practical method.

How are herb leaves dried on a screen?

There are commercially made driers, or you can make your own from old window screening. The screen must be elevated by wood, bricks, books, or something of the sort, so air will circulate under the screen as well as over it. Wash the leaves, blot them dry with a paper towel, and carefully remove them from the stems. Place them on the screen to dry, and turn the leaves once or twice to make sure they dry evenly.

Can I dry herbs in the microwave?

Yes. Put a single layer of herbs between two paper towels and dry for two minutes. If they are not yet dry, continue to microwave them for thirty-second intervals until they are brittle. For future reference, keep records of how long each variety of herb takes. Time varies with the type of herb and the microwave.

Can all herb leaves be air dried?

No, a few lose their color or flavor when air dried. The flavors of chervil and chives are best preserved by freezing. Fennel and burnet have no flavor when dried, and thus must be frozen. Parsley and dill can be stored for a short time wrapped in a moist paper towel and placed in the refrigerator.

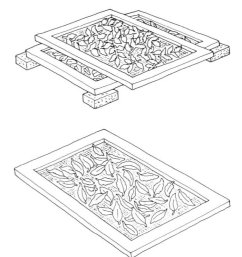

Place herb leaves on old window screens, elevated to ensure good air circulation.

Which herbs freeze best, and what is the procedure?

Basil, burnet, chervil, chives, dill, fennel, parsley, and tarragon can be frozen. Burnet, chervil, fennel, parsley, and tarragon benefit from being blanched in boiling water for one minute and then cooled in ice water before being wrapped and frozen. Others need only be washed. Remove the leaves from the stems, wrap them in aluminum foil or place them in plastic bags, and put them in the freezer. It is more convenient if you package them in amounts you are likely to use at one time.

I have a friend who stores herbs in the freezer in ice cube trays. How is this done?

Place 2 cups of the herb in a blender with 1 cup of water and blend well. Pour the mixture into ice cube trays and freeze. The cubes can be removed from the trays and stored in the freezer in plastic bags for quick and fresh seasoning for soups and stews.

I love pesto but have eaten it only when fresh basil is abundant. Can it be frozen?

Pesto freezes very well. A very special seasoning for pasta, soup, or potatoes, pesto must be made from fresh basil. A typical recipe is 1 ½ cups fresh, crushed basil combined thoroughly with ¾ cup grated parmesan cheese, 2 crushed cloves of garlic, and ¾ cup of olive oil. Many pesto recipes also call for ½ cup of pine nuts, pecans, walnuts, almonds, or cashews.

When should herb seeds be harvested?

The seeds are usually mature enough for harvest several weeks after the plants have flowered. Check them frequently to be sure you get them before they fall to the ground. Often their color changes to tan or gray. Choose a dry day, and cut the stem as long as possible.

How are seeds cured and dried?

In a dry spot with good air circulation, hang or place the stems upside down in a paper bag. As the seeds mature and fall from the plant, they will fall into the bag. Be sure the seeds are dry before you store them. To complete their drying, if necessary, spread them out on a fine screen or piece of cheesecloth.

What is the best method of storing dried herb leaves and seeds?

Leaves and seeds must be stored away from light and heat, in airtight containers so they do not absorb moisture. Placing them in clear glass jars on a spice rack over the stove is the worst thing you can do to them. Herbs can be stored for a week or so in the refrigerator if you wish.

Should leaves be stored whole, or can I chop them up first?

Leaves will retain more flavor if they are stored whole and broken up or ground when needed.

A few weeks after I stored my herbs, I noticed condensation on the inside of the container. Could this have been avoided?

The herbs were not dry enough when you bottled them. Take them out of the container and dry them again for another day or two or they will deteriorate.

How long will dried herbs keep?

That depends on the herb and how it is stored. If it has no scent, crush some of the leaves together, and if it still has no scent, it will have no flavor and should be discarded.

DRYING HERB FLOWERS

•

I would like herb flowers for dried flower arrangements and potpourris. When should I cut flowers for drying?

Most flowers dry best if they are cut when they are about one-third open. Check the listings in Chapter 5 for specific advice about individual flowers. Do not cut flowers that are wet from rain or dew.

How are flowers best dried?

Dry them by hanging them upside down or placing them on screens, in the same manner you would dry herb leaves. Some flowers, particularly calendula, can be dried with a desiccant, such as silica gel.

How can I dry flowers with silica gel?

Place 2 inches of silica gel (sold at craft shops) in a cookie or cake tin or other sealable, airtight container. Lay the flowers on the silica gel, sideways or face up, depending on their shape. Sprinkle more silica gel over the flowers until they are completely covered. Cover tightly and dry for two days to a week. When the flowers are dry, gently pour off the silica gel and lift the flowers out, blowing or brushing away any particles that stick to the petals.

Are there desiccants other than silica gel?

Yes, you can use sand or borax, but the container should not be sealed and the process will take longer.

Which herb flowers may be dried?

The herbs most commonly grown for dried flowers are calendula, chamomile, chives, clary, horehound, hyssop, lavender, lavender cotton, safflower, tansy, and yarrow.

Lay flowers on silica gel, pour more silica gel over them until they are covered, then cover the container tightly.

When recipes call for dried herbs, how much fresh herb should I use?

Because dried herbs have lost their moisture, their essential oils are more concentrated than in a comparable amount of fresh herbs. Therefore, if you wish to use fresh herbs in a recipe that calls for dry herbs, double or triple the amount listed.

At what point in the preparation should herbs be added?

Herbs release their oil quickly when they are heated. If you are cooking a dish, such as a stew, that takes several hours, add the herbs during the last half hour. When preparing foods that cook quickly, put the herbs in at the beginning, or sprinkle them on top of the dish when it is completed.

I often see the expression *"fines herbes"* in cookbooks. What does this mean?

A traditional French herb mixture, *fines herbes*—chives, chervil, parsley, and tarragon (and sometimes other herbs)—are used to season sauces, soups, and cheese and egg dishes. Gourmet cooks believe the flavor of these herbs is enhanced in combination, more than if any of them were used alone.

Can you give me a recipe for herb butter?

Mix ¼ cup of minced fresh herb or 2 tablespoons of the dried herb of your choice with one ¼-pound stick (½ cup) of softened butter. Combine well, using a blender or electric mixer if you wish. Let the mixture stand at room temperature for a few hours, then refrigerate it overnight.

COOKING WITH HERBS
•

Is there any way to "hurry up" herb butter for a last-minute dinner?

Soaking dried herbs in hot water for a few minutes before mixing them with the butter will release their oils, and therefore flavor the butter more quickly.

Can I use herbs in cold spreads other than butter?

Yes, use herbs to pick up the taste of margarine, cream cheese, sour cream, cottage cheese, or mayonnaise.

I grew bee balm, calendula, chamomile, hyssop, lemon balm, and sage so I could make teas. What is the best way to proceed?

Teas can be made from fresh or dried herbs. You can use one herb or a mixture of several different flavors—experiment to find a taste you like! Preheat a teapot, place a teaspoon of dried herbs or a tablespoon of fresh herbs, into it, and add boiling water. Steep for about ten minutes, strain, and serve.

I made some herbal tea, but the flavor wasn't strong enough. Should I steep it longer?

It would be better to add more herbs—steeping it longer will probably result in a bitter taste.

I didn't steep my herbal tea too long, but it still was bitter. What was wrong?

Did you use a metal tea pot? Metal pots, even those made from stainless steel, will make the tea bitter. Always use china or glass containers for tea making.

What are the best herbs to use to flavor cold drinks?

Use the same herbs in the same proportion as for hot teas. Since it takes longer to get flavor out of an herb in cold liquid, prepare the cold drink twelve to twenty-four hours in advance, or to speed things up, steep the tea in boiling water and then chill it in the refrigerator, or faster still, the freezer.

I usually make apple jelly every fall. Is there any herb I could combine with it to make it special?

Make the jelly the way you normally do, but place two or three leaves of basil, lemon balm, mint, rose geranium, rosemary, sage, or thyme in the jars before you pour the jelly into them.

What is herbal vinegar, and how can I make it?

Herbal vinegar can be made with white, cider, or wine vinegar, flavored with the herb of your choice. Use white vinegar if you want to show off the color of herbs, such as chive blossoms or purple basil. Mix 1 tablespoon of dried herbs or ½ cup of fresh

Herbal vinegars and teas and home-made jellies are only a few of the culinary uses of herbs.

herbs with 2 cups of vinegar. Allow this mixture to stand in a covered glass jar in a warm, dimly lit place for four to six weeks. Strain out the herbs, and store the vinegar in a labelled glass jar or bottle.

What herbs can be used to make vinegar?

You can use one or a combination of the following herbs: basil, burnet, caraway, chive flowers, dill, fennel, garlic, lavender, lovage, marjoram, mint, oregano, parsley, rosemary, sage, savory, scented geraniums, tarragon, and thyme.

How is herbal vinegar used?

Use herbal vinegar in any recipe calling for vinegar: sauce, marinade, salad dressing, stew, or vegetable.

I understand borage flowers can be candied and used as decorations on cakes. How is this done?

There are several ways to candy flowers. One of the easiest is to brush beaten egg white on the flowers, and then lay them on wax paper and sprinkle them with powdered sugar. Dry in a sunny window (it will take two to three days), or in a 200° F. oven for half an hour. Flowers can also be candied by dipping them in a sugar solution, and then sprinkling them with granulated sugar.

Candy borage flowers by brushing them with beaten egg white and sprinkling them with powdered sugar.

Is it possible to make homemade candied angelica for Christmas baking?

Yes, it's quite simple if you use a candy thermometer. Cut the stems into small pieces, and simmer them in a solution of 2 cups of sugar in 2 cups of water for twenty minutes. Drain the pieces, saving the sugar solution, and put them in the refrigerator, covered, for several days. Put the angelica back into the sugar syrup and heat it again for twenty minutes at 238° F., using a candy thermometer to check the temperature. Drain and dry. Store in airtight containers. Licorice-flavored candied angelica is an old-fashioned Christmas treat.

Herb-scented soap is delightful. Can you describe how to make some with homegrown herbs?

The easiest way is to make a semi-liquid gel by first grating any pure, mild, unscented soap. Next, boil 1½ cups of the desired herb, such as ground chamomile or lavender flowers, or the whole leaves of lemon grass or mint, in 6 cups of water for ½ hour. Cool and strain. To 3 cups of the scented water, add 2 cups of the grated soap and ½ cup of borax. Boil for 3 minutes and cool.

SCENTED CRAFTS FROM THE HERB GARDEN

•

To make a hard soap, grate a bar of unscented, pure soap. Add to it ¼ to ½ cup of water in which you have steeped 2 tablespoons of your favorite herbs. Mix well until it takes on the texture of molasses. Place it into molds or roll it into a ball with your wet fingers. Allow it to dry for several days. If you formed it into balls, turn them often so that they stay evenly round.

To make the soap smoother, you can heat the mixture in a double boiler over water.

What is potpourri?

Literally, potpourri means "rotten pot." Such an unpromising name, however, is actually a lovely mixture of dried flowers, leaves, essential oils, and spices, combined with a fixative, that retains its fragrance for many years.

What are essential oils?

These are the result of a distillation process that extracts an oil containing the distinctive aroma—the essence—of the plant. The distillation process is complex, so these oils are usually purchased from stores or mail-order companies that offer potpourri supplies (see Appendix). There are also essential animal oils such as ambergris, civet, and musk, used in making perfumes, but these are no longer available to the public, except in synthetic form.

What is a fixative?

A fixative aids in both preserving the leaves and petals, and retaining their natural scent. Angelica root, benzoin and gum storax, calamus root, orrisroot, and sandalwood are common fixatives. Orrisroot also seems to have a color-fixing effect, but you should be aware that some people are allergic to it. Fixatives, too, may be purchased where potpourri and dried flower supplies are sold.

What leaves and petals can be used for making potpourri?

The nicest thing about potpourri is that you can invent your own recipe by using any leaves or petals that have a pleasing fragrance. Some of the best, traditionally used ingredients are from the shrubs rose and jasmine; the annual and perennial flowers heliotrope, marigold, mignonette, stock, and wallflower; and the herbs geranium, lavender, lemon balm, lemon verbena, mint, rosemary, santolina, southernwood, thyme, and violet.

I want to make a potpourri of rose petals and herbs from my garden. How can I do this?

Pick fragrant rose petals (red holds its color best) when the flowers are in full bloom but not completely blown. Spread them carefully on sheets of paper, a screen, or strips of cheesecloth in a dry, airy room, away from the sun. Turn them daily. Let them dry completely—they should be crisp. This will take from a few days to a week, depending on the heat and the humidity. To each quart of petals, add 1 ounce of orrisroot as a fixative. Such herbs as lavender, lemon verbena, peppermint, rosemary, and thyme make wonderful additions to a rose potpourri, and you may also add, if you wish, one-half teaspoon each of such spices as cloves, cinnamon, coriander, and mace, along with a few drops of essential oil. Keep in an airtight earthen jar.

What is "wet potpourri," and how is it made?

Like the dry potpourri described in the previous question, wet potpourri contains rose petals, as well as petals of any other fragrant flowers that are available. First, partially dry the petals on fabric or paper, then pack them in layers in an earthenware jar, with a sprinkling of table salt or coarse salt over each layer, until the jar is filled. Add 1 ounce of orrisroot, an essential oil, and, if desired, some cloves, allspice, and cinnamon. Put a weight (such as a stone) on the petals and let them stand in the jar, covered, for several weeks before mixing. In addition to rose petals, scented geranium and lemon verbena leaves and lavender flowers and leaves are the most commonly used ingredients. Wet potpourri keeps its scent longer than dry potpourri.

I have heard that it is possible to make a potpourri that will repel moths. What is the recipe?

The basic, moth-repelling components can be lavender, lavender cotton, mint, pennyroyal, southernwood, or tansy. To make the scents pleasant to us, but not to moths, add cloves, lemon verbena, rosemary, or thyme. Use 1 ounce of chipped orrisroot per quart of petals as a fixative, and twice the amount of essential oil that you would add to other potpourris.

What herbs can I use to make holiday wreaths?

Silver King artemisia is the most commonly used base for a wreath, and lavender cotton is also good. Fresh southernwood makes excellent wreaths, which can be allowed to dry after they are fashioned. To the herbal wreath, add dried flowers of any kind for decoration. You can also make living wreaths of rosemary, sage, or thyme by filling a circular wire frame with sphagnum moss and inserting small plants into the moss. Place the live wreaths on a shallow tray in bright sun, and remember to water them regularly. These can be dried after the holiday season, if desired.

What is a tussie mussie?

A tussie mussie, or nosegay, dates back to the seventeenth century, when this tight bouquet of herbs and flowers was first used to deliver a message through the language of flowers. For

The silvery gray leaves of the artemisias are particularly fine in dried arrangements and wreaths.

Positive Images, Ivan Massar

Traditionally, tussie mussies were used to deliver messages through the symbolic language of flowers.

example, basil meant good wishes; borage, courage; burnet, merriment; rose geranium, preference; marjoram, joy; rosemary, remembrance; sage, good health; thyme, happiness; valerian, pleasure.

Make your own tussie mussie by arranging fresh herbs and flowers in a small bouquet and tying the stems together. Place scented geranium, lavender cotton, or tansy foliage around the flowers—and a paper doily under the flowers. Add colored ribbons for decoration. You may air dry it or dry it in silica gel.

Is there a way to scent our bathwater with herbs?

Scented bathwater is an old, and lovely, custom. Some nice herbs for this use include angelica, mints, rosemary, and thyme. You can simply add the fresh herbs to the bathwater or chop them and place them on a small piece of cheesecloth, which you can then gather into a bundle and tie with a ribbon. When they have "steeped" in the hot water for a few minutes, they will release a gentle, heady aroma for a delightfully relaxing bath.

What herbs are good for sachets?

Use dried mints, thyme, rosemary, sage, dill, lavender, sweet woodruff, or savory. You may wish to experiment with various combinations of these herbs. Let them sit in a closed container for the scents to marry, then grind them to a powder before filling your sachets.

Do you have any suggestions for how to cover sachets?

The coverings for sachets can be as simple as a pretty piece of calico sewn pillowcase fashion and gathered at the neck with a pretty ribbon. If you enjoy handcrafts, knit, crochet, or hand-weave your own fabric or use old table or bed linens, quilts, or old laces. If the fabric you choose has a loose weave or knit, make a muslin inner bag to hold the herbs so that they can't leak out.

How can I fix catnip for my cat to enjoy?

Follow the instructions on page 58 for harvesting and drying catnip. You can stuff the dried catnip into something as simple as a small fabric pillow, tightly machine-stitched closed, or use a purchased pattern for a small stuffed toy—mouse-shaped, if you wish.

What are lavender bottles, and how are they made?

An old English invention, lavender bottles are formed by bending fresh, blooming lavender stems back upon themselves, weaving the stems with ribbon to shape the "bottle," and then allowing it to dry. Lavender bottles may then be placed in drawers or hung in closets as moth repellents. To shape bottle, be sure to use only freshly picked lavender so that stems don't

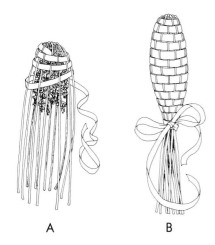

A   B

To make a lavender bottle (A) tie a thread around a bundle of stems just below the flower heads and gently bend stems down over the flowers; (B) weave ribbon through stems until flower heads are covered and fasten at the bottom with a bow.

break. Gather about fifteen stems and tie them tightly together with string just below the flowerheads. Holding the bundle with the flowerheads down, carefully bend each stem back down over the flowers. When all stems are down, weave 1/4-inch wide, velvet or satin ribbon between the stems until you have covered all of the flowers, tightening and smoothing the ribbon as you weave. You will need about 3 yards of ribbon. Tie a string around the stems at the base of the weaving and hang the bottle in an airy place until the lavender has dried thoroughly. You may need to tighten and smooth the ribbon, as the stems will shrink somewhat when they are dry. Wrap ribbon around the stems to hide the string. Decorate with bows.

5 Favorite Herbs to Grow

E ach herb has its own legend and lore, as well as specific characteristics and cultural needs. In this chapter, you will find descriptions, background information, and complete growing instructions for about sixty favorite herbs to enjoy in your garden. For further advice about the hardiness, height, uses, propagation, and light and soil needs of herbs, see the chart on pages 130-31. Hardiness zones (see page 2) are given for most herbs, and a zone map is included on page 132 for your reference.

Angelica (*Angelica Archangelica*)

Angelica sounds "heavenly." How did it get its name?

Angelica has been called "the herb of angels" because it was said to have been a gift from the angels to protect mankind from the plague.

What is angelica, and how is it used?

Angelica is a biennial that grows 5 feet tall and has large, aromatic, 2- to 3-foot, three-part leaves. It looks and smells a bit like celery. The leaves are used fresh or dry as seasonings, especially in drinks. The stems and leafstalks may be served in salads or as a vegetable, or they may be candied to decorate confections (see page 65). The seeds are used for flavoring and for oil, and the roots are sometimes dried and ground for use in baking.

◀ *The bright red blossoms of bee balm attract bees and hummingbirds to the garden.*

71

Ann Reilly

Angelica: The large leaves of this herb may be used fresh or dried to flavor beverages.

Can I grow angelica in my southern Vermont garden?

Yes, you live on the northern boundary of angelica's hardiness range, which is Zone 4. Angelica is fairly resistant to heat and will grow anywhere through Zone 10. It should be given winter protection at the edge of its hardiness zone.

I planted angelica for the first time last year, and it did not flower. Did I do something wrong?

No, but because angelica is a biennial, it will not form the large, flat or round clusters of greenish white flowers until early in its second summer.

How should I grow angelica?

Angelica prefers full sun or light shade, and fertile, moist, cool, well-drained soil, rich in organic matter. Feed plants with all-purpose plant food in early spring when growth starts. Mulch around the plants in mid- to late spring to keep the soil moist and cool. When plants are 1 foot high, pinch them back to keep them bushy (see page 27). Where winters are windy, stake or protect the tops of the plants to avoid damage.

Can I propagate angelica from seeds?

Yes, you can. Sow seeds indoors in early spring after storing them in moist sphagnum peat moss in the refrigerator for six to eight weeks. Germination will take twenty-one to twenty-five days. Move plants outdoors in mid-spring after the soil has warmed up, setting them 3 feet apart. You can also plant angelica seeds outdoors in fall, at a depth of ¼ to ½ inch, for germination the following spring. If you do not harvest angelica, the seeds will drop and readily self-sow. Angelica can also be propagated by root division in early spring.

This spring I tried to sow some angelica seeds that a friend gave me two years ago, but they did not germinate. What went wrong?

Angelica seeds are very short-lived and must be sown as soon as possible after they are harvested. The seeds you used were too old to germinate.

How should I harvest angelica?

Being careful not to damage the stem, pick the leaves in the fall of the first year or in the spring of the second year before the plant flowers. The leaves can be used fresh, or they can be dried in a cool, dark, dry, well-ventilated place. To harvest seeds and roots, you will have to forsake harvesting leaves and stems. Cut off the flower heads as the seeds start to turn light beige, and hang the flower clusters upside down in a paper bag in a dark, cool, dry area. Roots can be dug as soon as the seed heads are removed.

Anise *(Pimpinella Anisum)*

I have heard that anise has an ancient history. Is this true?

Yes, it was one of the herbs used for payment of taxes by the Romans, who brought it from Egypt to Europe. Anise, with its licoricelike flavor, soon became popular for use in bread, cookies, cake, and candy. Now, both leaves and seeds are used not only in baking but also as a flavoring in soups, salads, and Italian sausage. If anise is chewed after a meal, it is said to aid digestion and to sweeten one's breath.

What does anise look like?

With small, lacy leaves and flat clusters of yellowish white flowers, anise is a dainty, spreading plant that grows 18 to 24 inches high and blooms in early summer.

When can I plant anise into the garden?

Anise is a hardy annual that can be moved into the garden in early to mid-spring, as soon as the soil can be worked. Plants should be spaced 6 to 9 inches apart.

I would like to try propagating my own anise plants instead of buying them this year. Is that possible?

Anise is easily propagated from seeds. You can either start them indoors in late winter or sow them outside, ⅛ inch deep, as soon as the soil can be worked in spring. They will germinate in twenty to twenty-eight days. Anise does not like to be transplanted, so if you start seeds indoors, sow them into individual peat pots that can be planted directly into the ground without disturbing the roots. Seeds are short-lived and should not be saved from one year to another.

What care should I give to anise in the garden?

Anise should be grown in full sun in a dry, light, sandy soil. This herb should not be overwatered, so water only when the ground starts to become dry. Incorporate fertilizer into the soil before planting, and no other seeding will be necessary. Because stems are weak and may become leggy, stake them or mound soil around the base of the plants to give support.

How should I harvest anise?

Anise leaves can be picked from the plant at any time and used fresh or dried. To dry them, lay them on a screen in a dark, dry, cool, well-ventilated area. Harvest seeds after they mature, which is two to three weeks after flowering has ceased, when they are grayish brown. Cut off the flowering stem, tie stems in bunches, and hang them in a cool, dark place inside a paper bag. Be sure seeds are dry before storing them in an airtight container.

Anise: The licoricelike flavor of anise is popular in breads, cookies, cakes, and candies.

Maggie Oster

Anise hyssop: The leaves of anise hyssop make a nice addition to potpourri.

Anise hyssop *(Agastache Foeniculum)*

Is anise hyssop a cross between anise and hyssop?

No, it isn't, and it does not look like either plant, although its flavor is similar to anise and it is in the same botanical family as hyssop. It is a perennial, hardy to Zone 3, and grows 3 to 4 feet tall. Stems are square; leaves are oval, pointed, and sharply toothed; and flowers, which bloom in summer, are purplish blue.

How has anise hyssop been used?

The Plains Indians used anise hyssop leaves as a tea, sweetener, and medicine; the roots were used for coughs and colds, although it is no longer considered safe for culinary use. The leaves make a nice addition to potpourri.

Is anise hyssop easy to grow?

Yes, it is very easy to grow. In fact, it can become somewhat weedy because its roots spread quickly, and it self-sows easily. Grow it in full sun or light shade in sandy, well-drained soil. If the soil is rich in organic matter, growth will be even more rampant. It needs little fertilizer, but if you must apply some, do so in early spring.

How is anise hyssop propagated?

Anise hyssop can be grown from seeds sown at a depth of ½ inch either indoors or in the garden. Seeds germinate in seven to ten days. Propagation may also be accomplished in spring or fall by division, or by cuttings taken and rooted in summer. Space plants 18 inches apart.

How is anise hyssop dried?

Cut individual leaves or entire stems before the flowers appear. Dry them on a screen, or hang the stems upside down in a cool, dark, dry area.

Artemisia *(Artemisia* species)

How should I treat artemisia in the garden?

Grow it in full sun in well-drained soil. Although it does best in a good garden soil, it will tolerate soil with little organic matter, and either wet or dry soil conditions. Fertilize with bonemeal each year when growth starts.

Can the artemisias be grown from seeds?

They can, but the seeds are very fine and should therefore be sown indoors, not outdoors. They need light to germinate, so should not be covered. Germination will occur in seven to ten days. Move the plants into the garden four weeks before the last spring frost, and set them 18 inches apart.

What other method of propagation can I use besides seeding?

Divide artemisia plants in spring or fall, or take stem cuttings during summer.

I have seen reference to Silver King and Silver Queen artemisias in catalogues. Could you describe them please?

These are cultivars of *A. ludoviciana*, which is sometimes called Western sage. Plants are perennial and grow 2 to 3 feet high. The aromatic leaves of Silver King are narrow and silvery, while those of Silver Queen are wider, grayer, and downier. They are both very drought resistant.

How are these artemisias used?

Besides being very attractive mounded garden plants, these artemisias are used for wreaths and other handicrafts. Both the foliage and the yellow flowers, which are cut for drying just as the flowers start to open, will last for many years.

Silver King artemisia: This popular artemisia is excellent when dried for use in wreaths and arrangements.

Is Sweet Annie another cultivar of that species?

No, Sweet Annie is a tender annual artemisia, *A. annua*. It grows 6 feet or more high and has highly fragrant, green foliage that turns red in the fall. It is also used in wreaths, dried arrangements, and sachets.

What does wormwood look like?

A perennial hardy through Zone 2, wormwood (*A. Absinthium*) grows 3 feet tall and has gray, hairy, deeply divided leaves and inconspicuous yellow flowers in late summer.

Is wormwood the same plant that was used to flavor absinthe?

Yes, it is, but because of its harmful effect on the nervous system, this drink is illegal throughout the world. While wormwood should not be ingested, its dried leaves are one of the most effective moth repellents for stored clothing.

Wormwood: The dried leaves of wormwood make a very effective moth repellent.

Is southernwood related to wormwood?

Yes, southernwood (*A. abrotanum*) is a closely related species, with the same cultural requirements. However, whereas wormwood is a gray, sprawling plant, southernwood is bushy, green, and lush. Wormwood spreads rapidly underground, while southernwood does not. Southernwood is available in a variety of lovely fragrances—lemon, tangerine, and camphor.

How should I harvest wormwood?

Cut the stems in late summer, leaving a few inches of stem for winter protection. Remove the woody portion of the stem and dry only the green, upper portion by hanging the stems upside down in a dry, cool, well-ventilated spot.

Basil *(Ocimum Basilicum)*

I have always liked the taste of fresh basil in pesto and other Italian dishes, as well as in a variety of sauces and soups, but is it attractive enough to use in the garden as an ornamental?

Yes, both green- and purple-leaved varieties are lovely in the flower garden, and they bloom all summer until frost, with white to purplish flower spikes on 18- to 24-inch stems. The purple-leaved variety blends well with yellow-flowered annuals. A variety called Spicy Globe forms perfectly round, neat, 12-inch mounds of tiny foliage and flowers late in the season, if at all, making it an excellent border plant in both herb and ornamental gardens.

Basil: Spicy Globe basil makes an excellent border plant, with its round, neat, 12-inch mounds of tiny foliage.

Ann Reilly

How can I propagate my own basil plants?

Basil is a tender annual, propagated from seeds. It can be started indoors in spring, six to eight weeks before the last frost. The seeds will germinate in seven to ten days. Transplant the young plants outdoors after all danger of frost has passed. Seeds can also be sown outdoors, ¼ to ½ inch deep, after the danger of frost is over. Space plants 10 to 12 inches apart in the garden.

Is basil easy to care for in the garden?

Relatively easy. Grow it in full sun in a light-textured, well-drained soil, with a moderate amount of organic matter. Water it when the soil starts to dry out, and keep it evenly moist but not overly wet. To avoid leaf spotting, apply water to the ground and do not wet the leaves. If fertilizer is mixed into the soil before planting, no other feeding will be necessary. When plants are 4 to 6 inches tall, pinch them to encourage bushiness (see page 27). Basil likes warm soil, so apply a mulch in early summer.

I grew basil last year, but the plants were killed by an early frost before I got a chance to harvest the leaves. Is there anything I might have done to save them—other than harvesting early?

Yes. Basil is one of the first plants in the garden to be affected by frost. If an unexpected early frost is predicted, cover the plants at night with a clear plastic container or hot cap (see page 44). Plants can be treated in the same way if a late frost threatens to damage the plants in spring.

I picked my basil after the plants had started to flower and they didn't seem to have much flavor. Was it the variety?

Leaves harvested after the plants flower are not as flavorful. If you pinch out the flowers as soon as they appear, you will extend your period of harvest, allowing you to pick leaves throughout the summer. Be careful when you pick basil leaves, as they bruise easily, another cause of flavor loss.

What is the best way to dry basil leaves?

If you want to dry basil leaves for use in the winter, place them on a screen in a warm, dry, dark, airy place, freeze them (see page 61), or steep them in oil or vinegar.

Can basil be grown indoors?

Yes, it can. It is best to start new plants from seeds for the indoor kitchen garden, and grow them under lights or in a sunny window.

Basil: This standby of Italian dishes thrives in full sun in well-drained, moderately rich soil.

Are there any legends connected with basil?

Even though to many Westerners basil is synonymous with pasta and Italian cooking, some Hindus consider it sacred, believing that it makes the passage to heaven easier.

Bee balm, Bergamot (*Monarda didyma*)

I have heard that there is some association between bee balm and the American Revolution, but I can't recall the details. Can you tell me about this?

When colonists protested the use of the English tea tax by instigating the infamous Boston Tea Party and foreswearing the use of English tea, they satisfied their craving for tea by brewing bee balm leaves. Because this beverage was introduced to them by New York Oswego Indians, it was called Oswego Tea.

I am looking for an herb that will add some color to my garden. Can you suggest one?

Bee balm is an excellent choice, for not only does it have interesting and colorful red, pink, purple, salmon, or white flowers in early summer, but it also attracts bees and hummingbirds. This 2- to 4-foot perennial is hardy through Zone 4. Its hairy, somewhat coarse leaves have a minty fragrance.

My garden is lightly shaded. Can I grow bee balm?

Yes, it will grow well in full sun or light shade.

How can I start bee balm plants?

Bee balm can be grown from seeds or from cuttings. Start seeds indoors, as long as you can provide a temperature of no more than 55° F. for germination. Seeds will sprout in fifteen to twenty days. It may be easier to start seeds outdoors, sown ¼ to ½ inch deep, as soon as the soil can be worked in spring. Plants can also be divided in early spring or early fall and replanted 12 inches apart.

I grew bee balm last year, but it soon grew into the lawn and became a nuisance. What can I do?

The roots of bee balm, being related to mint, travel rapidly underground and can be invasive. Install a metal or brick edging to help control its growth. Plants tend to die out in the center, as the strong, young growth travels out from the original plant, so lift plants each year and replant the newer, outside pieces where you want them.

How are bee balm leaves dried?

Leaves can be dried on a screen, but they lose a lot of their flavor when dried and are therefore better used fresh.

Beefsteak plant. See Perilla

Bergamot. See Bee balm

Borage (*Borago officinalis*)

Is borage an annual or a perennial?

Borage is a hardy annual, which readily self-sows. It is easily grown from seed planted outdoors in fall or very early spring. Seeds sown in fall will germinate the following spring; seeds sown in spring will sprout in seven to ten days. Because borage is very difficult to transplant, starting it indoors is not recommended. Outside, sow it where it will grow, in full sun or light shade, ½ inch deep, and thin it to 12 inches between plants. Plants grow 2 to 3 feet tall and bloom all summer.

What are the uses of borage?

Young leaves may be used in salads, but mature leaves are coarse and hairy, and may be toxic if ingested often, in large quantities. The blue or purple, star-shaped flowers are pretty floated in drinks and punch bowls, or candied for use on cake, ice cream, and other desserts (see page 65). Both the leaves and the flowers have a cucumber flavor.

What is the history of borage?

Known from Roman times as a symbol of courage, Christian Crusaders were often toasted farewell with a borage-garnished drink.

I have fertile soil, rich in organic matter, but my borage doesn't grow well. What might be wrong?

Borage, like some other herbs, prefers dry, infertile soil, with no added organic matter.

My borage plants look unattractive by midsummer. What can I do?

To keep borage attractive, pinch plants back when they are 6 inches tall to encourage bushiness (see page 27). In midsummer, prune them back by one-half. They will produce a new crop of tender leaves that can be harvested in late summer.

Burnet *(Poterium Sanguisorba)*

I find raw cucumbers hard to digest, but I love the flavor of cucumbers. Are there any herbal substitutes?

Yes, the leaves of burnet taste very much like cucumbers, and should cause no digestive problems. They can be picked at any time throughout the season, and are particularly nice in salads and iced drinks. The leaves have no flavor when dry, but keep both their color and flavor when stored in vinegar. They may also be frozen.

What does burnet look like?

Burnet is a pretty plant, with finely cut leaves that are bunched in a 6-inch clump at the base of the plant. Gracefully arching, 18- to 24-inch stems are covered with small, toothed leaves. Dense tufts of white or rose-pink flowers bloom in early summer to midsummer. Burnet is a very hardy perennial, withstanding temperatures as cold as Zone 3. Its leaves stay green and flavorful even when covered with snow.

What growing conditions does burnet need?

Burnet likes full sun, but in hot climates it will need light shade. Soil should be alkaline, infertile, sandy, and well-drained, with no additional organic matter. Keep the ground dry.

I have had problems dividing burnet. Any suggestions?

Burnet has a long tap root and is thus very difficult to divide. If you want to try it, do so either in early to mid-spring or early fall. You will have better success if you propagate by seed. Start seeds indoors any time from early spring through early summer, and move plants into the garden up to six weeks before the first fall frost. Alternatively, sow seeds directly outdoors, any time from mid-spring up to two months before the first fall frost. Plant seeds ¼ to ½ inch deep. They will germinate in eight to ten days. Final spacing for plants should be 15 inches.

Burnet: The leaves of burnet taste very much like cucumber.

Maggie Oster

I like burnet, but it becomes weedy in my garden. What can I do?

Burnet easily reseeds and does in fact become weedy. Remove flowers as they start to fade to prevent seeds from dropping and sprouting.

Calendula, Pot marigold (*Calendula officinalis*)

I know that calendula is often called pot marigold. Is it a form of marigold?

Marigolds are distant relatives of calendula, but although gardeners in Shakespeare's time thought they were the same plant, they are not. Sixteenth-century gardeners grew them in pots, which is how they got their name.

Can I plant calendula in my flower garden?

Absolutely! Their pretty, daisylike flowers of orange, yellow, apricot, off-white, or gold are double, and the petals are crisp. Plants grow 6 to 24 inches high.

How is calendula used?

Calendula flower petals may be used for garnishes in soups and on hors d'oeuvres, in rice as a substitute for saffron, in butter for coloration, and in herbal teas, as well as in potpourri. Petals lose their slightly bitter flavor quickly, but retain their color.

I tried to grow calendula last summer in my Virginia garden, but it did not do well. Can you suggest why not?

This hardy annual likes cool climates but does not tolerate heat. Because Virginia summers are too hot for it, try growing it in the spring or fall. Be sure your soil is fertile, well-drained, and rich in organic matter, and keep it well watered. You should be able to grow it in either full sun or light shade. Fertilize prior to planting and again when flower buds start to form. A mulch applied in early spring will help to keep the soil cool and moist, and thus help prolong the life of calendula.

How should I propagate calendula?

Calendula can be propagated by seed, either indoors or directly in the garden. Germination will take ten to fourteen days. Indoors, start seeds six to eight weeks before you wish to plant them outdoors, whether you are planting in spring or fall. Cover the seeds completely, as they need darkness to germinate. Outdoors, sow seeds ¼ to ½ inch deep, in early spring, as soon as the soil can be worked. In mild areas, sow seeds in late summer for fall and winter bloom. Space plants 12 to 15 inches apart.

Maggie Oster

Calendula: The flower petals of calendula, or pot marigold, may be used as a soup or salad garnish.

Should I remove the petals from the flower heads of calendula before I dry them, or should I dry the flowers whole?

It doesn't matter—either method works equally well. Pick flowers as soon as they are fully open and dry the petals or the entire flower on a screen in a warm, dry, well-ventilated place. Petals may also be used fresh.

Caraway *(Carum Carvi)*

I'm familiar with the thin, crescent-shaped seeds of caraway in breads, rolls, cakes, and cookies, but what are the other uses of caraway?

The finely cut, dark green leaves may be used fresh in salads. The tap root, which looks like a white carrot, is edible and very nutritious. In ancient times, caraway was used as a medicine.

I planted caraway last spring, but the plant never developed flowers or seeds. What happened?

Caraway is a very hardy biennial (Zone 3), which, when sown in the spring, does not flower and set seed until the second summer. If sown and germinated in the fall, it will flower and set seed the following summer.

Does caraway fit well into the flower border or knot garden?

Caraway grows 2 to 2½ feet tall and can be rangy in growth, so it is not an appropriate plant for knot gardens or formal flower gardens. Its flat clusters of white flowers are lovely, however, in informal herb or flower gardens. It blooms in summer.

How is caraway grown?

Sow caraway seeds outdoors, ⅛ inch deep, in early fall to have flowers and seeds by the following summer. Thin the plants so that they are 6 to 9 inches apart. Caraway is very difficult to transplant; thus, sowing seeds indoors is not recommended. You will have greatest success if the soil does not have much organic matter. Also, do not water much, as this tends to keep the stems soft and causes the blossoms to fall before setting seed. Dry, sunny weather favors this crop, as does a light fertilizing prior to planting and again when growth starts in spring.

Can I harvest leaves, seeds, and roots from the same plant?

Yes. Leaves can be harvested at any time but are best when young and tender, and used fresh. After the flowers bloom and the seeds have turned brown, cut off the seed heads and hang them upside down in a plastic bag in a cool, dark, dry place. Then, dig up the plant for its roots. Roots can be harvested earlier in the year, but at the expense of the seed crop.

Ann Reilly

Caraway: A hardy biennial, caraway grows about 2 feet tall, with clusters of flat, white flowers.

My caraway seeds are covered in a fluffy chaff. How can I remove it?

You can either sift seeds through a ¼-inch mesh screen, or drop them, in a thin stream, into a bowl outdoors on a breezy day so that the chaff blows away.

Catmint. See Catnip

Catnip *(Nepeta Cataria)*

I would like to try growing catnip to make toys for my cats, but how can I keep the cats out of the garden while the catnip is growing?

Grow plants from seeds planted directly in the garden so that the fuzzy, gray-green foliage—which contains the oil that attracts the cats—is not bruised during transplanting. Bruising the leaves releases the scent, and once cats find this treat, you won't convince them to keep away from it. They are likely to trample neighboring plants as well as the catnip when they revel and roll in it.

I would like to grow catnip from seeds. What are the best procedures?

Start your seeds indoors any time in early spring through early summer, and transplant them into the garden in spring through late summer, up to six weeks before the first fall frost. Choose a soil that is dry, with little organic matter, in full sun or partial shade, and space plants 18 to 24 inches apart. If it's more convenient, you can also sow seeds directly into the garden during spring or summer, up to two months before the first fall frost. Plant them ¼ inch deep. Germination takes seven to ten days.

Will catnip return year after year?

Yes, catnip is a very hardy perennial (Zone 3) if the stalks are left on the plant and the plant is mulched. It is a very rapid grower and may need dividing every year to keep it within bounds. A metal edging around the plant will also help to contain it. Every year in the spring cut off the old, dead growth to improve its appearance. Fertilize little, if any, so that you don't encourage even heavier growth than normal.

Will catnip bloom more than once a year?

As soon as the first flowers fade, cut the plants back by half to encourage catnip to rebloom. The first blooming of the white to light purple, spiked flowers appears on 2- to 4-foot stems in early summer.

Catnip: Cut back plants after they flower to encourage a second period of bloom later in the summer.

When should catnip leaves be picked?

For the heaviest aroma, pick leaves before the flowers bloom. After drying them on a screen in a cool, dry, well-ventilated place, chop the leaves or rub them with your fingers to release more scent.

What is the difference between catnip and catmint?

Catmint *(Nepeta mussini)* is a different species of the same genus and thus closely related to catnip. Catmint has the same cultural requirements as catnip, and it also attracts cats, although it does not make them act as outlandishly.

Chamomile *(Chamaemelum nobile; Matricaria recutita)*

What is the difference between the two chamomiles?

They share many characteristics, although one is an annual and one is a perennial. Roman chamomile *(C. nobile)* is a perennial, hardy through Zone 4. A creeping, 6-inch plant that has lacy, gray-green foliage, it makes a fine ground cover. The tiny, strongly scented, daisylike flowers, which bloom in late summer, have yellow centers and white petals, although the petals are often missing. German chamomile *(M. recutita)* is an annual. The foliage and flowers are similar to Roman chamomile in appearance, but German chamomile grows 2 to 2½ feet tall, and blooms all summer if it is not too hot. Unlike Roman chamomile, the foliage of the annual carries an apple scent and makes a better-tasting tea.

Is there any difference in the uses of the two chamomiles?

The flowers of both chamomiles are used in making teas. The flowers of perennial chamomile are sometimes used as a hair rinse by blondes.

Are the two chamomiles grown in the same way?

Both prefer full sun or light shade and sandy, well-drained soil, with little organic matter. If the soil is too rich, few flowers will form. Once plants are established, both tolerate drought and excessive moisture, and neither likes hot summers. Both self-sow readily if flowers are not removed. The one area of difference is spacing: Perennial chamomile should be spaced 3 to 4 inches apart; annual chamomile, 8 inches apart. Perennial chamomile used as a ground cover can be cut with a lawn mower in early spring to encourage fuller growth.

Are both types of chamomile propagated the same way?

Both chamomiles can be propagated from seed. If sowing is done indoors, a temperature of 55° F. must be maintained. Seeds germinate in seven to ten days. Move plants into the garden

Positive Images, Jerry Howard

Chamomile: Pick flowers when they are in full bloom, but before they start to fade.

when they are young, because the long roots that older plants develop make transplanting difficult. Seeds may also be sown outdoors in spring as soon as the soil can be worked. Sow them ¼ to ½ inch deep. Perennial chamomile can also be propagated from cuttings.

How are the flowers harvested and treated?

Pick the flowers of both chamomiles when they are in full bloom, but before they start to fade. Dry them on a screen placed in the sun. Watch out for insects that hide in the flowers, and if you see any, pour hot water over them and start the drying procedure again.

Chervil *(Anthriscus Cerefolium)*

What is the flavor of chervil?

Chervil has a slight anise, or licorice, flavor. It is rarely used alone, but is an ingredient of *fines herbes*, a French culinary staple. It can be used in place of parsley in soups, stews, sauces, and salads.

Is there any use for chervil's flowers and seeds?

Chervil has flat clusters of white flowers that bloom on 24-inch stems in early summer, but only the finely divided, light green leaves are used as seasonings. Once the flowers bloom, the plants usually die back.

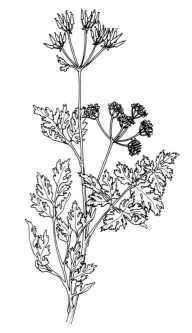

Chervil: The delicate leaves of chervil have a mild licorice flavor.

How is chervil grown?

Chervil is a hardy annual that is propagated from seeds, with germination taking seven to fourteen days. Seeds may be started indoors in winter, but because chervil does not like to be transplanted and may bloom prematurely if disturbed too much during transplanting, sow seeds into individual pots. Move plants outside as early in spring as the soil can be worked, setting them 6 to 8 inches apart. Seeds may also be sown outdoors in early spring or early fall, ¼ inch deep.

How should I treat chervil in the garden?

Light to full shade is beneficial. Soil should be sandy, well-drained, and evenly moist, with a lot of organic matter. Chervil grows well only when the night temperature is below 55° F., so it is often grown as a spring or fall plant, or as a winter plant in the south. Mulch the soil to keep it cool. Chervil self-sows readily if the flowers are not removed.

Does chervil need a lot of fertilizer?

If all-purpose fertilizer is incorporated into the soil before planting, no further fertilizing will be needed.

Is it true that chervil leaves can be frozen?

Yes, chervil leaves can be used fresh or frozen.

Chives *(Allium Schoenoprasum)*

Can chives be grown from seeds or must I buy plants?

They can be grown from seeds, but buying plants is much easier. Outdoors, sow seeds ¼ inch deep early in the spring through midsummer; indoors, sow them from late winter until early summer. Germination will take ten to fourteen days. Move plants outside any time after the soil is workable in spring, and space plants 6 to 8 inches apart. Chives can also be divided in early spring or early fall.

Are chives interchangeable with onions?

This onion relative can be used in any recipe that calls for raw green onions, though the chive flavor is more delicate. They are also well-loved mixed with sour cream, chopped into soups, and used with eggs and fresh tomatoes. Even the onion-flavored, pinkish purple flowers can be used in salads and omelettes. Chive flowers steeped in white vinegar will impart their rose color and oniony flavor to the vinegar.

I'm looking for a plant for the perennial border that doubles as an herb. Any suggestions?

Chives are one of the leading contenders. Hardy to Zone 3, these plants grow only 8 to 12 inches tall and have globe-shaped clusters of flowers, surrounded by grassy foliage, in late spring.

Do chives need moist or dry soil?

Plant chives in moist soil, rich in organic matter, in full sun to light shade.

Can chives be grown indoors?

Yes, they can. Grow them on a sunny windowsill, and for best results, place them in the refrigerator for four weeks during the winter to simulate dormancy.

How can I dry chives successfully? Mine shrivel up and lose their flavor.

Chives do not dry well. Try freezing them instead (see page 61).

What are garlic chives?

Also known as Chinese chives, garlic chives *(A. tuberosum)* have a delicious, subtle garlic flavor, making them an excellent salt substitute for chicken, pork, and lamb dishes, as well as a variety of soups and stews. They are also used raw in salads.

Chives: The striking pinkish purple flowers of chives make them an ideal plant for the late spring perennial border.

Madelaine Gray

Their leaves are flat in contrast to the round leaves of regular chives, and their flowers are white and fall-blooming. They freeze well. Planted near roses, they are said to enhance the rose scent.

Cilantro. See Coriander

Clary sage *(Salvia Sclarea)*

Is clary sage related to the perennial flower salvia? They are similar in appearance.

Both annual and biennial clary sages are members of this family. Biennial clary sage forms a rosette of foliage in the first year, and 3-foot spikes of white or purple flowers in the second year.

How do I use clary?

The flowers can be dried and used in arrangements. The essential oil, similar in taste to culinary sage, is commercially extracted from clary.

How is clary grown?

Clary is propagated from seeds. Sow them indoors in late winter and transfer them into the garden in mid-spring. Set plants 12 inches apart. Seeds can also be sown outside in early spring or early fall, ¼ to ½ inch deep. Plants like full sun and a moist soil, rich in organic matter.

Clary sage: This plant likes full sun and a moist soil, rich in organic matter.

Comfrey *(Symphytum officinale)*

Why is comfrey known by such common names as boneset, bruisewort, knitbone, and healing herb?

In the past, comfrey had many medicinal uses: It was believed to heal broken bones, sprains, and bruises when applied to the body in a paste form; and it was used as a gargle, as a cure for bleeding gums, and in teas to relieve digestive problems. Currently, there is a great deal of controversy about the safety of comfrey. Some herbalists contend it has been safely used for centuries; others claim it is carcinogenic. Comfrey is a good addition to the compost pile, as it is thought to activate bacteria and be a good soil conditioner.

Is comfrey a perennial? What does it look like?

Comfrey is a coarse, hairy perennial, hardy through Zone 2. Plants grow 3 feet tall and have hollow, angular, hairy stems. There are leaves all along the main stem, with those that spring from the base of the plant growing up to 10 inches long and looking like donkey's ears; the upper leaves are smaller. The

Maggie Oster

Comfrey: Because of its invasive nature, comfrey is best grown in a bed by itself.

white, pink, or pale purple flowers are bell-shaped and nodding, and bloom in clusters in mid-spring; they often continue to flower throughout the summer. The roots are juicy—black on the outside and white on the inside—and grow 1 to 6 feet in length and 1 inch in diameter.

How should I grow comfrey?

Comfrey likes full sun to partial shade and average to rich garden soil that is kept evenly moist. Plants will grow in dry soil, but they will not be as vigorous. To start your own plants, grow them from seeds sown outdoors in fall or early spring, or from purchased or divided roots planted in early spring and spaced 3 feet apart.

I understand that comfrey can become quite invasive. Is this true?

Yes, and because of this it is best to grow it in a bed by itself. Any piece of root left in the ground will grow into a new plant. The plant also freely self-sows, which can be controlled by removing the flowers as soon as they start to fade.

How is comfrey harvested?

Pick the mature leaves as the flowers start to open and dry them on a rack or a screen. Roots can be dug in the spring or the fall.

Coriander *(Coriandrum sativum)*

Is it easy to grow coriander seed?

Yes, but because coriander does not like to be transplanted, you must start the seeds outdoors in early spring where plants are to grow, ¼ to ½ inch deep. Seeds will germinate in ten to fourteen days. Thin them to 8 to 10 inches apart.

I have been told that coriander has an unpleasant scent. Why grow it?

Although the scent of the fresh leaves and seeds can be unpleasant, when they ripen and are dried, they become very fragrant. The lemon-scented seeds look like white peppercorns, and are the featured flavor in dishes from a variety of nations, including Indian curries, Oriental stir-fry dishes, and Scandinavian breads and cookies. The leaves have a flavor not unlike a combination of sage and citrus, and are sometimes called cilantro.

Will coriander grow in my partially shaded garden?

No, coriander needs full sun. It also needs moist soil, and should be fertilized at planting time.

When can I harvest coriander leaves and seeds?

Harvest their leaves throughout the summer and dry them on a screen in a dark, cool, well-ventilated place. The white or pale pink flowers bloom in late summer on 30-inch stems; seeds form about three weeks later. Cut stems off in early morning and hang them upside down in a paper bag to collect the seeds.

Costmary *(Chrysanthemum Balsamita)*

Can I grow costmary from seeds? I have never seen them in catalogues.

No, costmary cannot be grown from seeds, for it seldom blooms, and when it does, seeds usually do not form. Costmary is a perennial, hardy through Zone 4, and must be grown from root divisions or cuttings in early spring.

What does costmary look like?

Similar in appearance to some chrysanthemums, costmary grows 2 to 3 feet tall, with aromatic, oblong foliage. When flowers do appear, they are daisylike, with yellow centers and white petals, and bloom in late summer.

Is costmary easy to grow?

Some gardeners would say it is *too* easy to grow, in fact, it can be weedy. It likes full sun, but will grow less vigorously in partial shade. It grows quickly, so space plants 3 feet apart and fertilize little, if any.

How is costmary used?

In the Middle Ages, before brewers started using hops, costmary was used in beer. It was once called "Bibleleaf" because early settlers used it as a bookmark in their Bibles and nibbled on it to keep awake during church sermons. Leaves have a spearmint flavor and can be used fresh or dried in salads, soups, and stews.

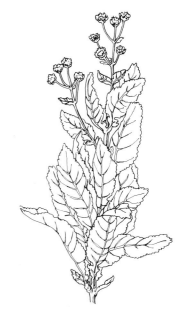

Costmary: A hardy, fast-growing perennial, costmary imparts a spearmint flavor to salads, soups, and stew.

Cumin *(Cuminum Cyminum)*

I tried to grow cumin last year in my northern Wisconsin garden, but the plants never flowered. Can you suggest why?

Cumin must have at least three months of hot summer weather to flower and set seeds. In areas with short growing seasons, such as northern Wisconsin, seeds must be started indoors before the last spring frost. Since cumin is a tender annual, set plants into the garden in full sun after all frost danger has passed. Where the growing season is long, sow seeds in the garden where they are to grow, ¼ inch deep. The plants need not be thinned too radically; if you space them about 6 inches apart, the weak 6-inch stems can support each other.

How long does it take for cumin seeds to germinate?

Seeds will sprout in ten to fourteen days.

Can cumin be grown in average garden soil?

Yes, average is fine, if it is well drained. Water when the soil starts to dry out. Incorporate fertilizer at planting time; no further feeding is necessary.

Can the leaves of cumin be used?

The threadlike *leaves* of cumin are not used in cooking, but the pungent *seeds* were used in Biblical times, and still continue to be used in Mexican, North African, Indian, and Portuguese dishes, in chili, curry, cheese, and sausages.

How should I harvest cumin seeds?

The seeds will mature about three weeks after the flat clusters of white or rose flowers appear. Cut the stems and hang them upside down in a paper bag to collect the seeds.

Dill (*Anethum graveolens*)

I often use dill seeds for pickles and dill leaves on fish. Did dill ever have any other uses?

Dill is taken from an Old English word that means "to lull" because it was once used to soothe cranky babies to sleep. Ancient superstition held that dill could be used to cast a spell to keep witches away.

I grew dill last summer, but the plant was unattractive and the stems fell over. What can I do?

The 2- to 3-foot tall stems of dill are naturally weak, and they get especially top-heavy when the flat clusters of yellow flowers appear in midsummer. Stake them or grow them close together (4 to 8 inches) so that they will support each other.

Is dill an annual?

Yes, it is a hardy annual, which means that it can be planted in the garden in early spring as soon as the soil can be worked.

I have not had success growing dill from seed. Any suggestions?

Indoors, dill seeds must not be covered when sown, as they need light to germinate. You can start them indoors in late winter, in individual pots because they resent being transplanted. They take twenty-one to twenty-five days to germinate.

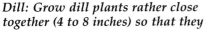

Dill: Grow dill plants rather close together (4 to 8 inches) so that they will support each other.

Madelaine Gray

Move plants to the garden as soon as the soil can be worked in spring. Seeds can also be sown outdoors in early spring, ¼ inch deep.

What parts of the dill plant can be used in cooking?

The finely divided, light green leaves may be used fresh or dry to season eggs, vegetables, fish, and sauces. Use the seeds for flavoring, especially for pickles. Seeds form following bloom in midsummer.

What care does dill need in the garden?

Provide dill with full sun and a well-drained, moist soil, with a moderate amount of organic matter. Fertilize prior to planting only. Dill self-sows easily and can become weedy unless seed heads are removed before the seeds drop. Do not plant it near fennel, as the two will cross-pollinate and the seeds will not be usable.

I am not interested in dill seeds, only the foliage. How can I increase my harvest?

Do not allow flowers to form. You can continue to pick the leaves at any time and use them fresh or dried. Leaves do not have much flavor if air dried. To store them for short periods, wrap them in a paper towel and place them in a paper bag in the refrigerator.

Are there any special techniques in drying dill seeds?

Cut the stems and hang them upside down in a paper bag. Unlike many other herbs, dill must be dried in a hot (90° F.) area.

Dittany of Crete. See Oregano

Fennel *(Foeniculum vulgare)*

Fennel's licorice-like flavor reminds me of anise. Are they related?

No. Actually, fennel looks much like a large dill plant, with threadlike, bright green foliage and flat clusters of yellow flowers in summer. It grows 4 to 5 feet tall.

How is fennel used?

Fennel leaves are used in soup, salad, and fish dishes. They do not retain their flavor when dried, so must be used fresh, or if desired, they can be frozen. Fennel seeds are used in bread, cookies, sauces, and sausages. Fennel stalks, eaten raw like celery, are said to reduce the appetite. They can also be placed on the barbecue to flavor fish when grilling it.

Maggie Oster

Fennel: This herb will continue to develop if you keep flowers from forming.

Is fennel an annual or a perennial?

Fennel is a tender perennial, but it is best grown as an annual for it is only slightly frost tolerant.

I have heard that there are some special considerations to be alert to when planting fennel in the garden. Can you explain?

If fennel is planted near dill, the two will cross-pollinate, and the seeds will be unusable. It will not grow well when planted near either coriander or wormwood, and it harms the growth of bush beans, caraway, tomatoes, and kohlrabi.

Do you have any historical information about fennel?

The ancient Battle of Marathon, which gave its name to the long-distance run, was fought in a field of fennel.

How is fennel grown from seed?

Because fennel does not transplant well, start seeds indoors in individual pots, six to eight weeks before the last spring frost. Seeds will germinate in ten to fourteen days. Move them into full sun in the garden after the last frost. After frost danger is past, seeds may also be sown outdoors, ⅛ inch deep, where they are to grow. Final spacing for plants should be 8 to 12 inches.

Is fennel fussy about soil?

Not really. It likes moderately fertile, alkaline soil, and tolerates a wide range of moisture levels.

How can I increase the harvest of fresh leaves of fennel?

Leaves will continue to develop, increasing your harvest, if you don't let flowers form. This, of course, means that there will be no seeds to harvest.

Are fennel seeds difficult to harvest?

They are a little more time-consuming to harvest than other herb seeds because all the seeds on a single stem do not ripen at the same time. One way to harvest them is to hold each flower head over a paper bag and knock seeds off gently every day or two. If this seems too time-consuming, wait until seeds start to fall, and then cut the stem and hang it upside down in a paper bag.

Garlic (*Allium sativum*)

Can garlic be grown from seeds?

Yes, but it is usually grown from the small bulblets called "cloves" that grow around the base of the main bulb. You can buy cloves in a garden center or just use garlic from the supermarket. Plant the cloves outdoors in mid-spring, just below the soil surface, 3 to 4 inches apart, and harvest them the following fall.

Can garlic be grown in Florida or other areas where summers are hot?

Yes, it can, but because it doesn't like excessive heat, it will grow better if it is planted in the fall and harvested in the spring.

I see that garlic is a member of the onion family. Does it resemble onions in its growth habits?

It looks a lot like other *Alliums*. The leaves are long, narrow, and flat, and the white flowers bloom in globular clusters on 3-foot stems in midsummer. Small bulblets may be found within the flowers. Unlike some *Alliums*, it will not withstand freezing weather.

Is garlic of any use in the vegetable garden?

Interplanting garlic between other plants is an excellent way to conserve space, and garlic also helps to deter cabbage moths, Japanese beetles, and aphids.

Are the care requirements of garlic the same as for vegetables?

Yes, garlic likes full sun and moist, sandy, fertile soil, with moderate amounts of organic material.

Garlic: Full sun and moist, sandy, fertile soil are preferred by this popular herb.

How do I know when garlic is ready to be harvested?

When the foliage starts to turn yellow at the end of the season, bend the tops over (without breaking them off) to speed up ripening and drying. Leave the bulbs in the soil for two to three days, then dig them up and let them dry in the sun. Braid the tops together and hang them in a cool, dry, well-ventilated spot. Save several bulbs for cloves for next year's crop.

Garlic chives. See Chives

Geraniums. See Scented geraniums

Germander *(Teucrium Chamaedrys)*

How is germander used in the garden?

Because it is an evergreen shrub only 10 to 12 inches high and can be kept closely clipped, germander is used primarily as a decorative edging in herb gardens, especially knot gardens. It has small glossy leaves, and flowers in late summer with loose spikes of purple or rose-colored flowers, which are often removed to maintain the neat shape of the plant and keep the pattern of the planting intact. This herb was once thought useful to alleviate gout.

What are the cultural requirements of germander?

Although it tolerates partial shade, heat, and poor, rocky soil, germander will be best and densest in full sun and well-drained soil, rich in organic matter. It is hardy through Zone 5, but will need winter protection in Zones 5 and 6 to keep the tops evergreen and alive.

Can I grow germander from seeds?

Yes, seeds can be sown indoors or outdoors, planted ¼ inch deep. They take twenty-five to thirty days to germinate. Germander seedlings grow very slowly, however, so if you propagate by division or take stem cuttings you will have plants more quickly. Set plants 12 inches apart in the garden.

Ginseng *(Panax Quinquefolius)*

I have always thought of ginseng as an exotic herb. Can I grow it in my New Jersey garden?

Ginseng has centuries of mystery surrounding it, perhaps more than any other herb. It has been used and esteemed by the Chinese for its perceived medicinal, restorative, and aphrodisiac qualities. The roots are used to make a tea with a strong, bitter flavor. Ginseng is a woodland plant hardy through Zone 3, but it will not grow in areas that do not have freezing weather during the winter.

Can you describe ginseng to me?

It is a perennial, growing 15 to 18 inches tall, with whorls of five-part leaves and small clusters of greenish white flowers. Early summer-blooming flowers are followed by red berries.

Is ginseng easy to grow?

Growing ginseng is a challenge as its growing requirements are very stringent. It must have light, fertile, well-drained soil that is slightly acidic and rich in organic matter. Keep the soil constantly moist; enrich it with woodland material such as leaf mold; and use a low-nitrogen, slow-acting fertilizer such as bonemeal. A summer mulch will help keep soil moist as well as cool. Grow in full shade, preferably in deep woods where it will be cool and moist. Apply a protective mulch in winter.

I saw ginseng seeds listed in a seed swap. Is it easy to grow from seed?

No, growing plants from seed is as challenging (if not more so) as growing the plants themselves. Seeds cannot be started indoors. Rinse seeds in a 10-percent bleach solution before sowing them outdoors in the fall, ½ inch deep. They may germinate the following spring, although sometimes not until

Ginseng: Long recognized as a Chinese tea, ginseng must be grown in a woodland setting.

the second spring. It is easier to root plants from cuttings in spring, planting them 1 inch deep. After rooting occurs, space plants 15 inches apart.

How should I harvest ginseng?

In the fourth or fifth year, dig up the roots carefully. Wash them with water and dry them on a rack or screen in a warm, well-ventilated spot. It may take four weeks for them to dry completely.

Heliotrope. See Valerian

Horehound (*Marrubium vulgare*)

How did horehound get its name?

Horehound was used years ago as a remedy for dog bites. Today, the flowers and leaves are used to brew a tea said to relieve coughs, and it is the major ingredient in an old-fashioned candy; it is also one of the bitter herbs used in the Passover seder.

I planted horehound for the first time last summer, but it did not bloom. Is this normal?

Yes, it is. When grown from seeds, this perennial, hardy to Zone 3, often does not produce its whorls of tubular, white flowers until the second summer.

Will you describe the appearance of horehound?

Horehound is a spreading plant that grows 18 to 24 inches high. Square, gray, downy stems are covered with deeply veined, woolly, aromatic leaves.

How is horehound propagated?

Horehound can be grown from seeds sown outdoors from as early in spring as the soil can be worked until two months before the first fall frost. Plant seeds ½ inch deep; they will germinate in ten to fourteen days. Thin the plants to stand 8 to 10 inches apart. Because horehound is difficult to transplant, starting seeds indoors is not recommended. Division, too, although possible in mid-spring or early fall, can also be difficult. Rooting cuttings in spring or summer works well.

How can I keep horehound from becoming rangy and spindly?

Plant horehound close together to help the weak stems support each other. Every few years, divide and replant, or take cuttings and discard the original plant. For strongest growth, plant horehound in full sun.

Maggie Oster

Horehound: A spreading plant, horehound does best in full sun.

What type of soil does horehound require?

Horehound prefers average, sandy, well-drained soil, but tolerates poor soil and dry conditions, as well as a wide range of soil acidity. Fertilize plants each year when growth starts.

When should I harvest horehound?

Pick flowers and leaves when the plants are in full bloom. Dry them on a screen in a cool, dry, well-ventilated spot. The flowers are very sticky to handle.

Horseradish *(Armoracia rusticana)*

Is horseradish a more potent form of radish?

No. Although they are in the same plant family, they are not of the same genus (the next biological grouping under family).

What does horseradish look like?

Horseradish is a large, coarse plant with leaves sometimes 2 feet long and tiny, white flowers that appear in June. The plant is grown for its pungent roots, which may be as long as 2 feet.

Will horseradish grow in my Missouri garden?

Yes, it is a perennial, hardy through Zone 4.

How do I propagate horseradish?

In spring or fall, cut pieces of the root into 2- to 8-inch long sections, and plant them 1 foot apart and 6 to 12 inches below the soil surface. Horseradish rarely sets seed, and even when it does, the seed is hard to find.

Can horseradish become invasive?

Yes, it can. Confine it to a section of the garden where you want to grow nothing else. No matter how hard you try, it is impossible to remove all pieces of root from the soil, and even the smallest part of a root will grow into a new plant.

Ann Reilly

Horseradish: The pungent roots of horseradish may be as long as 2 feet.

What type of growing conditions should I give to horseradish?

Horseradish likes full sun or partial shade and a deep, rich, moist, loose soil, rich in organic matter.

When should I harvest the roots of horseradish?

Dig up the roots in the fall of the second year; after that, they may become bitter and grainy. If you store the roots whole and grate them as you need to use them, you will get a stronger flavor. Beware, however—fresh, homegrown horseradish can be very "hot" indeed!

Hyssop *(Hyssopus officinalis)*

Is the hyssop we grow today the same kind of plant that was mentioned in the Bible?

No one knows for sure, but it's possible. We know that in the Middle Ages it was strewn on floors to give the house a fresh, clean smell. Today, it is used as a flavoring in liqueurs, in a tea thought to relieve sore throats and coughs, and as a border or hedge plant in formal herb and knot gardens.

Is hyssop a perennial?

Yes. Hardy through Zone 3, hyssop grows 18 to 24 inches tall and has aromatic, dark green leaves and spikes of blue-violet flowers in summer.

Does hyssop require special care?

Hyssop likes dry, well-drained, alkaline soil. It grows well in full sun or light shade, but not where winters are warm. For best results when fertilizing it, use fish emulsion. With these conditions supplied, it is easy to grow.

How is hyssop propagated?

Hyssop may be propagated from seeds, by division of the roots, or by stem cuttings. Sow seeds ¼ inch deep indoors in early spring or outdoors in early spring or fall. Germination will occur in seven to ten days. Divide plants in spring or fall, and take cuttings in summer.

How far apart should hyssop be spaced?

In the garden, space plants 18 inches apart; as a hedge or in a knot garden, 12 inches apart.

When should I harvest hyssop?

Pick leaves and flowers when the plant is in full bloom, and dry them on a screen in a dry, well-ventilated place.

Hyssop: This herb is equally fine in the garden as a neat border plant and for culinary use as a flavoring or a tea.

Lavender *(Lavandula angustifolia)*

What is the care and use of lavender?

Lavender grows well in a dry, sunny place, in any light, well-drained soil that is not too acid. Cut dead branches back in the spring after new growth near the base is fairly strong. Lavender is grown for both ornament and fragrance. The blue-violet flowers that bloom on 18- to 24-inch spikes in early summer are used in perfumes, potpourri, soaps, aromatic vinegars, and sachets. The aromatic, gray-green, needlelike leaves are attractive in the garden.

Ann Reilly

Lavender: Grown for both ornament and fragrance, lavender does best in a dry, sunny place, in any light, well-drained, non-acid soil.

How can I make lavender plants produce more bloom?

Lavender gives much more prolific bloom, and better fragrance, if grown in a light, well-drained soil, high in lime content. Heavy soils or soils too rich in organic matter encourage foliage growth rather than bloom, and fertile soils produce flowers that are not fragrant.

When should lavender flowers be harvested?

Pick flowers when they are about to open, and dry them on a screen or upright in a vase in a dark, airy place.

Can lavender grow and live over winter as far north as Boston?

It should, if it is given good winter protection, such as marsh hay or evergreen boughs. The soil must be well-drained, for excessive moisture in the soil in winter kills lavender more than the cold does. Even with protection, plants three years old or more have a way of dying back in winter.

How can I start lavender from seed?

Seeds germinate rather slowly, and the tiny plants grow slowly. Start seeds indoors in early spring after refrigerating them for four to six weeks. Set out the new plants after all danger of frost is past. As soon as buds appear the first year, cut them off to prevent them from blooming. Outdoors, sow seeds in fall, ½ inch deep; they will germinate the following spring.

Can I propagate lavender from cuttings?

Yes. In either late fall or early spring, cut 2-inch shoots, taking a little piece of the main stem—a "heel," or portion of older wood—attached to the base of the shoot. Remove lower leaves from cuttings for about 1 inch, and insert the cuttings in well-packed sand. Keep the sand moist. Slight bottom heat will encourage rooting. When roots are not more than ½ inch long, put cuttings in small pots in a mixture of half sand and half soil.

Lavender cotton *(Santolina Chamaecyparissus)*

Is lavender cotton related to lavender?

No, the two plants are not related. Lavender cotton forms a shrubby mound of aromatic, woolly, silver, fernlike foliage. Because it is easy to trim, it is often used in hedges and knot gardens. In summer, it has golden yellow, buttonlike flowers that are clipped off if the gardener wishes to control the plant's shape closely. Insects dislike the scent of lavender cotton, so it makes a good moth-repellent.

Is lavender cotton a perennial?

Yes, but it is hardy only through Zone 6. In cold areas, you can grow it as an annual.

What growing requirements does lavender cotton have?

Grow it in full sun. Although it prefers average, dry, well-drained soil, it is very tolerant of poor, sandy soil. It is also a good seashore plant as it tolerates salt spray. In regions where it would be only marginally hardy, protect it in winter with evergreen boughs or salt hay. To encourage new growth, cut plants back to 4 to 6 inches in spring.

What is the best way to propagate lavender cotton?

Plants are easy to grow from seeds sown either indoors or outdoors from early spring through midsummer. Sow seeds ¼ inch deep; they will germinate in fifteen to twenty days. Plants will flower the first year, if started early enough. Set plants into the garden 18 to 20 inches apart. Lavender cotton can also be propagated by division in early spring, by rooting stem cuttings in summer (though cuttings are slow to root), or by layering.

When should I harvest lavender cotton?

Pick leaves and flowers when the plant starts to bloom, and dry them on a screen in a warm, dry, well-ventilated spot.

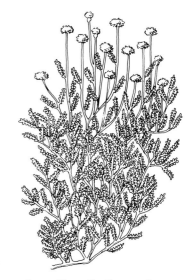

Lavender cotton: In the garden, lavender cotton forms a shrubby mound of aromatic, silvery foliage; dried, it serves as an excellent moth repellent.

Lemon balm *(Melissa officinalis)*

What are the uses of lemon balm?

Refreshing, lemony, hot and cold drinks can be brewed from lemon balm. In fact, in early England, longevity was credited to drinking lemon balm tea. It can also be used in jelly and fruit salad. The crisp leaves have more flavor when used fresh, although they can be dried. Lemon balm oil is used as furniture polish, but fresh leaves rubbed on wooden furniture also make a fine polish.

Can I grow lemon balm in my southern Florida garden?

Probably not. Lemon balm does not like hot, humid climates, although it will tolerate dry heat. It is a perennial, hardy to Zone 4.

Can lemon balm be grown from seeds?

Yes, it can. Start indoors in early spring, at least ten weeks before the last spring frost. Seedlings germinate in fourteen days, but they need a long time to become established. Do not cover the seeds, as they require light to germinate. Alternatively, you can sow seeds outdoors in early spring or early fall. Thin plants to 18 inches apart. Lemon balm can also be propagated by division or stem cuttings.

Will lemon balm grow in light shade?

Yes, it actually does best in light shade. It also likes light, sandy, moderately fertile, well-drained soil. Although it prefers moist soil, once established it tolerates drought.

Maggie Oster

Lemon balm: Brew refreshing, lemony, hot or cold drinks from lemon balm.

What other care requirements does lemon balm have?

After the white flowers bloom in summer, shear the plants back by half to stand about 12 inches high; this will keep them compact.

How should I dry lemon balm leaves?

Before the plants bloom, cut stems off at ground level and hang them upside down in loosely tied bunches in a dark, dry, airy space. Handle the leaves as little as possible during harvesting or drying as they bruise easily. In order for leaves to retain their green color, they must be dried at 90° to 110° F.

Lemon grass (*Cymbopogon citratus*)

What is lemon grass?

The blades of lemon grass, which can grow to 6 feet tall, are used commercially to distill a lemon-scented oil that is used in perfumes and artificial flavorings. Use fresh leaves in cooking or in tea, and dried leaves in potpourri. Cut leaves at any time for fresh use, or spread them on a screen to dry.

Can I grow lemon grass in my South Carolina garden?

Lemon grass is a tropical plant that will survive outdoors year-round only in the warmest parts of Zone 10. However, it can be grown as an annual in the ground or in containers, provided the summer is long and hot.

How should I grow lemon grass?

Give lemon grass a spot in full sun with sandy, well-drained soil. Keep it well watered. If container-grown, apply liquid fertilizer every two weeks. If planted in the ground, feed it once every two months during the growing season.

How can I propagate lemon grass?

Lemon grass rarely flowers and sets seed, so plants are propagated by division. Since it is seldom grown as a perennial in the United States, you will probably have to buy new plants each year.

Lemon verbena *(Aloysia triphylla)*

Is lemon verbena a perennial?

This open-growing shrub is hardy only in Zones 9 and 10. However, it may be possible to grow it in other areas of the country if you dig up the plant with its roots in fall, store it indoors over the winter, and replant it in spring after frost danger has passed. It must be confessed, however, that your chances for success with this procedure are limited.

How is lemon verbena used?

When dried, the lance-shaped, lemon-scented leaves retain their fragrance for many years in potpourris and sachets. In fact, their lemon scent lasts longer than that of any other lemony herb.

Can lemon verbena be grown from seeds?

No, it can't. Propagate it by rooting stem cuttings in summer.

Can lemon verbena be added to the flower garden?

Its lovely green foliage makes a fine accent plant in the June garden, but the spikes of white to lavender flowers that bloom in late summer are rather insignificant.

How is lemon verbena grown?

Plant it in full sun in sandy, moist, well-drained soil, rich in organic matter. Fertilize at planting time.

Can lemon verbena be grown indoors over the winter?

Some gardeners have luck growing lemon verbena indoors, particularly on an enclosed porch or in a plant window where the temperature is cool (55° F.). If you bring it inside and the leaves fall off, place the roots in a cool place and then move the plant outdoors in spring.

Ann Reilly

Lemon grass: The leaves of lemon grass retain their lemon scent unusually long in potpourris and sachets.

When should the leaves of lemon verbena be harvested?

Any time throughout the summer. Dry them on a screen in a cool, dark, well-ventilated spot.

Lovage *(Levisticum officinale)*

I understand lovage can be used as a celery substitute. Is this true?

Yes, lovage looks like celery, although it grows much larger—up to 3 feet high when it is not blooming and 6 feet high in bloom. Lovage and celery have many similar uses. The hollow stems may be used as a substitute for celery in soups; leaves, which, like seeds, are celery flavored, may be used fresh or dried in salads, soups, and stews; whole seeds, in baking; and crushed seeds, like celery powder.

Can I grow lovage in San Diego?

No. Lovage is a perennial that must have winter temperatures of at least as low as 20° F. (though no lower than 0° F.).

How is lovage grown from seeds?

Start seeds indoors in early spring in individual pots, as lovage does not like to be transplanted. Germination takes ten to fourteen days. You can also sow outdoors, ½ inch deep, in fall or spring. Be sure seeds are fresh, as they do not live long. Alternatively, you can divide plants in early spring or late fall, setting plants 12 to 15 inches apart, in full sun or light shade.

Should I add peat moss when improving the soil to grow lovage?

Yes, lovage likes a moist, well-drained soil, rich in organic matter. Fertilize yearly when growth starts and again in summer if leaves turn light green.

How should I harvest the various parts of the lovage plant?

For fresh leaves, cut off the outside leaf stalks. For dried leaves, cut the stem before the greenish yellow flowers bloom in summer. If you cut down the stems, there will, of course, be no seeds to harvest. Dry leaves on a screen in a warm, dry area or in a warm oven. As soon as seeds start to turn tan, harvest them by placing the seed heads upside down in a paper bag.

Marjoram, Sweet marjoram *(Origanum Majorana)*

Is marjoram a perennial or an annual? I have seen it listed both ways in books.

A member of the Mint family, marjoram is a perennial, but it is hardy only to Zone 9, so it is usually grown as an annual. It has

Maggie Oster

Lovage: A celery look-alike, lovage may often be used as a celery substitute.

Maggie Oster

Marjoram: Usually grown as an annual, marjoram is hardy as a perennial only to Zone 9.

oval, velvety, aromatic leaves and inconspicuous clusters of pink-ish white flowers in summer. Plants grow 8 to 10 inches high.

How is marjoram propagated?

Marjoram is grown from seeds, preferably indoors because the seeds are very small. Sow seeds in late winter (germination takes eight to fourteen days), and move the plants outdoors in mid-spring, setting them 6 to 8 inches apart. You can take cuttings in fall and grow plants indoors over the winter.

What growing conditions does sweet marjoram need?

Give marjoram a light, well-drained, neutral soil, with a moderate amount of organic matter, and full sun. Fertilize lightly at planting time.

How is marjoram used?

The leaves of marjoram are used fresh or dry in egg or tomato dishes and to flavor meat, vegetables, and salads.

How should I harvest marjoram?

Pick the leaves any time before the flowers bloom. You can extend the harvest period, in fact, by removing the flower buds as they form. Dry leaves on a screen in a warm, dry place, or hang stems upside down to dry.

Mint *(Mentha* species)

How is mint grown?

Mint grows best in deep, moist soil, rich in organic matter, in an open, well-drained spot, in either full sun or light shade. Fertilize lightly after plants are harvested. Mint can be invasive, so control it by thinning yearly or by inserting an underground barrier such as metal edging. Pinch off growing stems regularly to prevent the plants from becoming leggy.

Can mint be grown from seed?

Yes, it can, but plants, especially peppermints, do not come true from seeds and may vary in flavor from the parent. The best way to grow mint is from cuttings or divisions of a variety whose flavor you like. Take cuttings in summer or divide roots in early spring. Plants grow quickly and can be set 12 to 24 inches apart.

How is mint dried?

Peppermint is best for drying, although the fragrances and flavors of spearmint, orange mint, and apple mint also will last

Selected Culinary Mints

COMMON NAME	BOTANICAL NAME	CHARACTERISTICS
Apple	*M. suaveolens*	Hairy foliage; an especially decorative variety is pineapple mint *(Variegata)*; pineapple mint loses its flavor when dried, but apple mint actually improves
Corsican	*M. Requienii*	Creeping, tiny-leaved mint; strong flavor used for the liqueur *crème de menthe*; not winter hardy in most Northern regions
Horsemint	*M. longifolia*	Flavor resembles spearmint; tall perennial with long, gray, hairy leaves
Peppermint, or woolly	*M. x piperita*	Refreshingly flavorful; best mint for drying
Spearmint	*M. spicata*	Most common culinary mint; an attractive variety of *M. spicata* is curly mint

for years. Cut stems before the plant flowers and hang them upside down in a cool, dry, well-ventilated place. All mints may be used fresh in hot and cold drinks, salads, and jellies, or as a garnish.

Oregano (*Origanum vulgare*)

How can I determine what oregano is best to buy?

Dried oregano packaged to season Italian dishes does not come from one plant but is a mixture of dried herbs blended for their flavor. To further confuse things, there is some disagreement among botanists and herb experts as to what species is considered "garden oregano." Some common oreganos are *Origanum vulgare*, *O. virens*, and *O. dictamnus*. When you are selecting plants, to be sure you are getting the flavor you want, taste a tiny bit of the leaf or rub a leaf to see if it emits a strong, pleasant fragrance. Tasty oregano usually has clusters of white flowers, while less interesting ones have purple or pink flowers.

Can oregano be grown from seeds?

Yes, it can, but although some varieties may be to your liking, many of the plants lack flavor. Taste-test to find your preference, then take divisions or cuttings from your favorite plants. If you do start from seed, sow seeds indoors in late winter. Germination takes ten to fifteen days. Sowing seeds outdoors is not recommended. Move the plants to the garden after frost danger has passed, setting them in full sun, 12 inches apart.

What type of soil does oregano like?

Oregano likes a light, well-drained soil, with no added organic matter. Fertilize very lightly, if at all.

Is oregano a perennial?

Some species are. If you are uncertain, protect your plants over winter with a heavy mulch of leaves, evergreen boughs, or straw.

How should I harvest my oregano?

Cut the stems when they start to bloom, and hang them upside down to dry in a cool, well-ventilated, dry room.

What is dittany of Crete and how is it grown in the herb garden?

Dittany of Crete *(O. Dictamnus)* is an ornamental oregano with round, gray leaves. It may be started from seeds or by taking cuttings. Not hardy where winters are cold, it must be wintered indoors in pots. Provide it with sandy soil, perfect drainage, and full sun.

Maggie Oster

Oregano: For the best oregano, begin new plants from cuttings or division from taste-tested specimens.

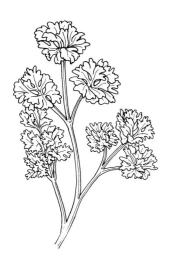

Curly-leaf parsley: This popular herb makes an especially attractive garnish.

Italian parsley: Known also as flat-leaf parsley, Italian parsley is considered by many to have a better flavor than the more familiar curly-leaf variety.

Parsley *(Petroselinum crispum)*

Is parsley a biennial or an annual?

Parsley is technically a hardy biennial, but it is usually grown as an annual because the foliage becomes tough and bitter the second year. If you grow it as a biennial, it will form flat clusters of yellowish green flowers late in spring of its second year.

I have read that parsley seed is difficult to germinate. Are there any tips you can give me?

Parsley is *slow* to germinate. In fact, a traditional saying maintains that it goes to the Devil and back nine times before it germinates. You can speed up germination, however, by soaking seeds in warm water for twenty-four hours before sowing; if this is done, seeds should germinate within twenty-one days. Another way to speed germination is to freeze seeds in ice cubes for three weeks before sowing.

Can I start parsley seeds indoors?

Yes, but because parsley does not like to be transplanted, sow seeds into individual pots. You may also sow seeds outdoors, ¼ inch deep, two to four weeks before the last spring frost. Thin plants to stand 6 to 8 inches apart. In mild areas, sow seeds outdoors in fall for harvest the following spring. Cover the seeds completely as they need darkness to germinate.

What type of soil does parsley need?

Parsley likes a deeply prepared, well-drained soil. Add generous amounts of organic matter to the soil when planting. Fertilize plants when they are 4 inches tall and again one month later.

Does parsley need full sun?

Parsley will grow in full sun or light shade.

How is parsley used?

Use parsley fresh or dried in almost any meat, fish, egg, or vegetable dish, or as a garnish. If used with garlic, it will cut the garlic aftertaste. Parsley is one of the ingredients of *fines herbes*.

How should parsley be dried? On my first attempt at drying it, the leaves lost their color.

Drying parsley on a screen usually results in loss of color. Try drying it on paper towels in a microwave oven (you will have to experiment cautiously for the required time, as that depends upon the size and power of individual ovens). You can also dry parsley in a slow-cooker set on low for overnight. It can be stored for a short time wrapped in paper towels and placed in the refrigerator.

Parsley did not do well in my summer herb garden in Phoenix last year. Can you suggest why?

Parsley does not like summer heat. If you garden where summers are hot, grow it in fall, winter, and spring.

Can parsley be dug in the fall and potted for winter use in the home?

Yes, it can, but because the roots are very long and deep, be careful when digging and plant it in a large pot. Better yet, sow new seeds or use very young plants for your windowsill garden.

Pennyroyal (Mentha Pulegium)

What is the difference between American and English pennyroyal?

English pennyroyal (*M. Pulegium*) is a perennial, hardy through Zone 3. A spreading plant with dark green leaves, it grows 6 inches tall. American pennyroyal (*Hedeoma pulegioides*) is an upright, annual plant with light green leaves; it grows 12 inches tall. Both American and English pennyroyal have pungent, citronella-like leaves and spikes of lavender-blue flowers in summer. Their growth needs and uses are identical.

How is pennyroyal used?

Pennyroyal got its name from one of its bygone uses—a body lice deterrent for British royalty. Although it is no longer used medicinally as it was in the past, it is one of the best herbs for repelling insects. It is also used in potpourri and tussie mussies.

Can pennyroyal be grown anywhere in the United States?

English pennyroyal can be grown as far north as Zone 3, although it will need winter protection in the northern limits of its hardiness. Neither the English nor the American pennyroyal likes extremely hot weather.

How is pennyroyal propagated?

Annual pennyroyal is propagated from seeds started indoors or in the garden, sown ¼ to ½ inch deep. It germinates in fifteen days. Because perennial pennyroyal is slow to germinate, it may be better to propagate it from division in either spring or early fall, or by rooting cuttings in summer. Space plants 12 to 24 inches apart.

Does pennyroyal need full sun?

Pennyroyal grows equally well in full sun or light shade.

Ann Reilly

Pennyroyal: Use pennyroyal as an insect repellent, or in potpourris and tussie mussies.

What type of soil does pennyroyal need?

Pennyroyal likes sandy, well-drained soil, kept constantly moist and rich in organic matter. Fertilize around it in early spring when growth starts and again after harvesting.

When should pennyroyal be picked?

Harvest pennyroyal before the plant flowers by cutting the stems to the ground. Hang the stems upside down in a dry, cool, well-ventilated place.

Perilla, Beefsteak plant *(Perilla frutescens)*

I have admired perilla growing in the Bahamas. Can I grow it in my New York garden?

If you grow it as a tender annual, you can. This very pretty plant has crisp, deeply cut, green or reddish purple foliage with a metallic sheen. Plants grow 18 to 36 inches high. You can grow it as a bedding plant for its foliage color or in the herb garden. It makes a colorful and striking addition when the fresh leaves are used in salads and with fruit. The fresh flowers are eye-catching added to fish or used in soup, stir-fry cooking, and meat and vegetable dishes.

What are the flowers of perilla like?

The lavender, pink, or white flowers bloom on spikes in early fall. Where growing seasons are short, the plants may not bloom.

I tried to grow perilla from seed last year, but did not have success. What happened?

Perilla has several specific growing requirements that you must meet. Do not cover the seeds in the sowing flat, for they must have light in order to germinate. Sow it in individual pots, because it is one of the herbs that does not like to be transplanted. Be sure to wait until all danger of frost has passed before sowing the seeds outside. Seeds germinate in fifteen to twenty days.

What kind of soil does perilla need, and how far apart should it be planted?

Soil should be dry and moderately rich in organic matter, with fertilizer added at planting time. Space plants 12 to 15 inches apart, in full sun or light shade. When the plants are 6 inches high, pinch the growing tips to encourage bushiness.

When can I harvest perilla?

Pick leaves and flowers at any time and use them fresh.

Ann Reilly

Perilla: The crisp green or reddish purple foliage of perilla makes a striking addition to the flower or herb border.

Pot marigold. See Calendula

Rosemary *(Rosmarinus officinalis)*

Are there any legends connected with rosemary?

Rosemary, a native of the Mediterranean region, is said to have gotten its name because the Virgin Mary hung her cloak on it when the Holy Family fled from Herod's soldiers to the safety of Egypt. Because of its associations with constancy and remembrance, its leaves have long been used in bridal bouquets and crowns. It is said to be a good hair rinse for brunettes. Legend aside, it is excellent with lamb and other meat dishes, as well as with poultry.

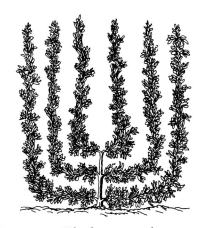

Rosemary: Whether grown in containers or directly in the ground, shrubby rosemary can be trained into various espalier forms.

Is rosemary a perennial? I have noticed it blooming in California in late winter.

A member of the Mint family, rosemary is a perennial shrub only in Zones 8 through 10. In colder areas, grow it as an annual, although if the growing season is not long enough, it may not bloom. Where it is hardy, it blooms with short spikes of pale blue flowers in late winter or early spring and grows as tall as 5 feet.

What is the best way to grow rosemary?

Grow it in light, well-drained, slightly moist soil, in full sun or partial shade. Space plants 12 to 18 inches apart. When rosemary is grown as an annual, fertilize it at planting time; when grown as a perennial, fertilize when growth starts in spring. Mist the foliage daily during hot weather, but be careful not to overwater this plant.

Can I grow rosemary from seeds in my Pennsylvania garden?

In your hardiness zone you would be better off buying plants or propagating rosemary from cuttings. Because it develops slowly from seeds, rosemary is best seeded only in warmer areas. If you start seeds indoors, provide a cool room (55° F.) for germination, which will take eighteen to twenty-one days. Plants can be set outside two to four weeks before the last spring frost. Outdoors, sow seed ¼ to ½ inch deep as early in spring as the soil can be worked.

When should I undertake the various methods of propagating rosemary if I don't start it from seed?

Divide established plants in spring of their second or third year, root stem cuttings in summer, or layer the branches by weighting an outside branch to the ground until roots form, also in summer.

Can I keep rosemary plants in a garden in Illinois from one year to another if I give them heavy winter protection?

No amount of winter protection will keep rosemary alive outdoors during an Illinois winter. You can try growing it in containers and bringing the containers indoors for the winter if you have a cool (55° F.) room or greenhouse. If you don't have space for large plants in the house, take cuttings and grow small plants indoors during the winter.

When can I harvest rosemary?

For fresh or dry use, cut stems back any time before the plant flowers. Dry leaves on a screen in a cool, dry, well-ventilated area, or hang stems upside down to dry.

Rue *(Ruta graveolens)*

Can I use rue in cooking?

Definitely not. Although rue is found in some old recipes, it is potentially harmful. It is a good insect repellent, but it is grown primarily for its decorative foliage, which is deeply cut, lacy, fernlike, and blue-green. It grows 1½ to 3 feet tall, and has buttonlike flowers that bloom in clusters in early summer to midsummer. Rue has a very strong aroma. The fresh foliage often causes dermatitis, so wear gloves when handling it.

Rue: Grown primarily for its blue-green, fernlike foliage, rue prefers full sun and a heavy, but well-drained, soil.

Maggie Oster

Is rue hardy in northern gardens?

Rue is hardy to southern New England, but in very severe climates it should be kept indoors during the winter or grown as an annual.

What are the cultural requirements of rue?

It prefers full sun, and heavy but well-drained soil, with little organic matter. Keep the soil evenly moist. Fertilize in early spring.

How can I propagate rue?

Sow rue seeds ½ inch deep, indoors in late winter or outdoors in early spring as soon as the soil can be worked. Germination will take ten to fourteen days. Move plants outside in early spring, setting them 6 to 12 inches apart. Plants can be divided in summer. Stem cuttings can be rooted, but this is the least successful means of propagation.

How should I harvest rue?

Because rue sometimes causes an allergic rash, wear gloves when picking the leaves. Spread the herb on a screen in a cool, dry, well-ventilated place. Once leaves are dry, they will no longer cause skin irritation.

Safflower *(Carthamus tinctorius)*

Why is safflower called "false saffron"?

True saffron, valued for both its subtle flavor and the golden color it lends to foods, is produced from a corm and it takes a large number of corms to produce a small amount of the herb. Safflower's thistlelike, deep yellow to orange, summer-blooming flowers can be dried, crushed into a powder, and used as a substitute for the rarer, and thus expensive saffron. Safflower may also be used as a dye for wool and, especially, silk, and its dried flowers are attractive in everlasting bouquets and in potpourris.

Safflower: The thistlelike, deep yellow blossoms of safflower may be dried and used as a substitute for the more expensive saffron.

Can I grow safflower in my sunny annual flower garden?

You can, but keep in mind that it has a coarse texture, with large, toothed, and hairy leaves. The plants grow 3 feet tall, so should be placed at the back of the border and spaced 12 inches apart. Grow safflower in average, well-drained soil; be careful not to overwater it.

Can safflower be grown from seeds?

As a matter of fact, this is the only way to propagate safflower. Sow seeds indoors 8 weeks before the last spring frost, sowing in individual pots since safflower is very difficult to transplant. You can also wait until after all frost danger has passed, and sow seeds outdoors where plants are to grow, planting them ¼ inch deep. Seeds germinate in ten days.

When should I pick flowers for drying?

Pick flowers as soon as they are open and before they start to fade. Dry them on a screen in a warm, dry, well-ventilated place, or, if you plan to use them only for ornamental purposes (not culinary), in silica gel. Store flowers, either whole or ground, in an airtight container.

Saffron (*Crocus sativus*)

Saffron is so expensive at the market. Is it possible to grow my own?

Yes, you can grow saffron, but it will be difficult to grow enough plants to produce any sizable amount for the kitchen. Saffron is produced from a corm (a modified stem filled with food storage tissue; similar to a bulb), related to spring-flowering crocus and very similar to it in appearance. The three central orange or red stigmas (part of the flower's female reproductive system) are harvested, ground into a powder, and used to color and flavor such foods as bread and rice. Because it takes several hundred plants to produce enough saffron to fill a tiny container, you might want to consider growing safflower (see entry above).

Is saffron grown the same way as crocus?

It is similar, except that saffron flowers in the fall. Plant saffron corms in early fall, 3 to 4 inches deep and 3 to 4 inches apart, in full sun or light shade and well-drained, moist soil, rich in organic matter. Plants will bloom the same fall they are planted and every fall thereafter in Zones 6 through 10. Do not remove the foliage, which lasts all winter, until it turns completely brown in the spring. Fertilize plants when the foliage turns brown or when growth restarts in fall. At the edge of its hardiness limit, apply a heavy winter protection.

Can saffron be grown from seeds?

No. Instead, in fall or early spring, when plantings become crowded, or if flowers diminish in number, dig up the saffron and divide it by pulling off the cormels (tiny new corms) that form around the base of the original corm. Replant the new cormels immediately, but discard the mother corm, as it will not grow again.

How can I produce powdered saffron?

Pick the flowers in the early morning as they start to open. Remove the orange or red stigmas from the center of the flower

Saffron: Produced from a corm, saffron resembles spring-flowering crocus.

and dry them in a warm, dry, well-ventilated location. When they are dry, grind the stigmas, and store the powder in an airtight container.

Sage *(Salvia officinalis)*

Which kind of sage should I grow for culinary use?

The sage used in poultry stuffing, sausage, Italian veal dishes, cheese, and tea, is *S. officinalis*. Tricolor is an attractive cultivar of *S. officinalis*, with variegated leaves of green, white, and purple. Pineapple sage *(S. elegans)* has pineapple-scented foliage and red flowers. Although it is not winter hardy, it can be grown as an annual. A closely related herb is clary (see page 87). Both are members of the Mint family.

I have been unsuccessful in growing sage. What are its needs?

Sage enjoys a well-drained, light, sandy soil. It prefers average to moist growing conditions, but must have dry soil during the winter. Plant it in full sun or light shade. Fertilize plants each spring as growth starts, and at the same time, prune plants

Sage: Leaves may be harvested several times over the course of the summer.

Maggie Oster

back to encourage bushiness. It is quite hardy, through Zone 3, and should not need winter protection unless winters are very harsh.

What are the best propagation methods for sage?

Start plants from seeds sown either indoors in late winter or outdoors in early spring, ½ inch deep. Germination takes fourteen to twenty-one days. Because plants are slow to develop, however, propagation is usually done by division in spring when growth starts. You can also root stem cuttings in late spring, or layer them in early fall by weighting down an outer branch with a rock until the branch takes root; transplant the new plant the following spring. Space plants 12 to 18 inches apart.

My sage plants are quite large. Can I cut them back severely when harvesting leaves this fall?

Not unless you live in a warm climate. If you cut off more than ⅓ of the plant in the fall, sage may be susceptible to winter damage. Wait until spring to cut it back heavily.

When can I pick leaves for drying?

Pick leaves before the plant blooms in late spring and early summer, and again in late summer. Tie the stems into bundles and hang them upside down to dry, or strip leaves from the stems and dry them on a screen in a warm, well-ventilated, dry place.

Scented geraniums *(Pelargonium* species)

My scented geraniums do not have the blooms that my garden geraniums do.

Both are of the genus *Pelargonium,* but they are different species, or subgroups, of that genus. Scented geraniums are

Selected Scented Geraniums

COMMON NAME	BOTANICAL NAME	HEIGHT	DESCRIPTION
Finger bowl	*P. crispum*	3 feet	Pink flowers; small, lemon-scented leaves
Fragrant	*P. x fragrans*	12 inches	Trailing plant; white flowers; nutmeg-scented leaves
Lemon	*P. x limoneum*	2 feet	Purple and lavender flowers; lemon-scented foliage
Nutmeg	*P. odoratissimum*	18 inches	Trailing plant; white flowers; apple-scented foliage
Oakleaf	*P. quercifolium*	4 feet	Rose-purple flowers; almond-scented leaves
Peppermint, or wooly	*P. tomentosum*	3 feet	White flowers splotched in red; velvety, mint-scented foliage
Rose	*P. graveolens*	3 feet	Rose-colored flowers; rose-scented foliage

Madelaine Gray

Scented geraniums: Rose and other scented geraniums make good garnishes for drinks, jellies, and fruits.

characterized by fragrant foliage, and their loose clusters of small flowers are secondary, although they do bloom lightly during summer. Their delicious scent is released in the hot sun and by rubbing the leaves. Fresh leaves may be used in baked goods, cold drinks, and jellies, as well as to garnish fruit; dried leaves may be used in teas and potpourris.

Are scented geraniums annuals?

Technically, they are perennials, but they are hardy only in Zones 9 and 10, so plants are usually grown as annuals.

Can I propagate scented geraniums from seeds?

Yes, you can, but sowing seeds is often not as successful as rooting cuttings. Seeds must be started indoors twelve weeks before the last spring frost, and germination is slow—up to fifty days. Move plants to the garden after the last frost. Starting seeds outdoors is rarely successful.

How can I root scented geraniums from cuttings?

Take stem cuttings from new growth in summer and root them in peat moss and perlite or sand (see pages 34-35). Pinch them when they are young, to encourage compactness.

What type of soil do scented geraniums prefer?

Rich, light, well-drained soil. Water plants when the soil starts to dry out, but be careful not to overwater. When the plants are growing or flowering, fertilize monthly with houseplant fertilizer.

When can scented geranium leaves be picked for drying?

Pick them at any time to use fresh, or dry them on a screen in a dark, cool, well-ventilated place.

Can I grow scented geraniums indoors over the winter?

Yes. You can either bring entire plants indoors, or root cuttings in late summer and grow them indoors over the winter. Rooting new cuttings each year will give more satisfactory results, as old plants tend to get woody and do not grow well. Grow scented geraniums in full sun or under lights, fertilize monthly, and water when the soil dries out.

Sesame *(Sesamum indicum)*

Does the command "open sesame" from the Arabian Nights have anything to do with the herb sesame?

Yes, it probably was inspired by the fact that the ripened pods of sesame burst suddenly to expel the seeds. Egyptians and Persians were familiar with the plant and ground its seeds for flour. Ground sesame seeds are still used in Near East cooking. The nutty seeds are often found in a variety of cakes, cookies, breads, and bagels, and they are the main ingredient of benne wafers, a Charleston, South Carolina favorite.

Can I grow sesame in my Alabama garden?

Yes, your climate would be ideal. Sesame is a tender annual and needs a long, hot growing season of at least 120 days to flower and set seeds. Sesame would probably not grow well in regions colder than Zone 7.

Does sesame make a good garden ornamental?

Yes, it does. Plants, which grow 2 to 3 feet tall, have long, pointed, dark green, slightly hairy leaves and spikes of bell-shaped flowers in summer.

How can I grow sesame from seeds?

Sesame seeds can be started indoors or outdoors, but where hot summer weather lasts less than four months, seeds must be started indoors. Sesame does not like to be transplanted, so seeds must be started in individual pots. Germination takes five to seven days. Move plants outdoors after frost danger has passed, setting them 6 inches apart. Where seeds can be sown outdoors, sow them ¼ inch deep after frost danger has passed and nights are above 60° F.

Does sesame require any special care?

No, give it full sun and average soil. Fertilize at planting time, and water when the ground starts to dry out.

Sesame: A warm-climate plant that requires a long, hot growing season, sesame thrives in full sun and average soil.

How do I harvest seeds without losing them?

Cut the mature pods *before* they burst open by cutting the stems off at ground level and placing them upside down in a paper bag.

Southernwood. See Artemisia

Summer savory (*Satureja hortensis*)

What is the difference between summer savory and winter savory?

Summer savory is a hardy annual, while winter savory (see page 127) is a perennial. Both, however, have linear, gray-green leaves and loose spikes of white, pink, or pale lavender flowers in summer. Summer savory is bushy, growing 12 to 18 inches high, and winter savory is spreading, growing 6 to 12 inches high. Both have a peppery flavor, but the flavor of summer savory is more delicate and is an excellent substitute for sage in poultry stuffing. Use either summer or winter savory fresh or dry to flavor meat, beans, and other vegetables. If you put summer savory in the cooking water, it will cut the odors of cabbage, turnip, and other strong-smelling vegetables.

What kind of soil culture does summer savory need?

Summer savory grows best in a moist but light, sandy soil, with little organic matter. Choose an exposed sunny site. Never allow the soil to dry out. Fertilize at planting time; no further feeding is necessary.

I started seeds of summer savory indoors last year, but they did not do well when I transplanted them. What was wrong?

Summer savory does not like to be transplanted, so use individual pots when sowing seeds indoors. Because the very small seeds need light to germinate, do not cover them with planting medium. Seeds germinate in ten to fifteen days. Move plants to the garden, placing them 4 to 6 inches apart, four weeks before the last spring frost. You can also sow seed outdoors in early spring as soon as the soil can be worked. Make a succession of plantings for a continuous harvest.

Why should I make successive plantings of summer savory?

Because summer savory must be harvested by cutting the entire stem back just before the plants bloom, planting summer savory every two weeks (known as succession planting) will ensure a continuous supply all summer and fall. After you have cut the stems, tie them in bunches and hang them upside down to dry in a warm, dry, well-ventilated place.

My plants of summer savory were quite spindly last year. Will fertilizing them more help?

Feeding may actually make them *more* spindly, because it encourages stem and leaf growth. Because "leggy" growth is normal for summer savory, you may wish to set plants close together so that they will support each other.

Sweet Annie. See Artemisia

Sweet cicely *(Myrrhis odorata)*

Can I grow sweet cicely in my North Dakota garden?

Yes, sweet cicely, a perennial herb hardy to Zone 3, would survive North Dakota winters. In fact, it prefers northern climates, especially if you can provide it a shaded, woodland garden with soil rich in organic matter.

What does sweet cicely look and taste like?

With its soft, fernlike foliage and small, white flowers, it looks much like a large version of chervil. It grows quickly, reaching a height of 2 feet in May. The leaves, stems, and seed pods, which taste like anise, may all be eaten.

I tried to grow sweet cicely from seed last year, but it didn't germinate. What did I do wrong?

Sweet cicely seed needs stratification, or cold treatments (see page 25), before it will germinate. If you want to start this plant indoors, place seeds in moistened peat moss in a covered container in the refrigerator for two to three months before sowing. After sowing, germination will take thirty days or more. To begin sweet cicely outdoors, sow *fresh* seeds ½ inch deep, as soon as they form in the fall: they will germinate the next spring.

I understand sweet cicely is difficult to transplant. Is this true?

Yes, it is. Because sweet cicely has a long tap root, it does not like to be moved. When growing seedlings, sow them into individual pots or transplant them when they are very small. Mature plants are difficult to divide, and are best propagated by cuttings.

How is sweet cicely used?

Eat the licorice candylike seed pods of sweet cicely fresh. Use leaves fresh or dried in teas, with vegetables, or as a substitute for anise or fennel. Place stems of sweet cicely on the barbecue coals when grilling fish.

Maggie Oster

Sweet cicely: This perennial herb prefers northern climates and shaded, woodland gardens.

Sweet flag *(Acorus Calamus)*

What is sweet flag?

A perennial, hardy through Zone 3, sweet flag is a waterside plant that looks like grass or cattails, with its fragrant, sword-shaped leaves growing 1½ to 6 feet tall. It is grown for its rhizomes (underground, horizontal root stocks).

How is sweet flag used?

Its dried root, also called calamus root, is used as a fixative in potpourri (see pages 66–67). Some American Indians used sweet flag for fever, coughs, colds, and toothaches; others believed it brought courage when rubbed on the skin. During the Depression, it was used as a substitute for chewing tobacco, but it is now considered carcinogenic.

I want to grow sweet flag in my herb garden. Does it need full sun?

Full sun is not necessary for sweet flag, although it will grow in full sun. If it is not grown by the water, it must have moist soil, rich in organic matter.

How is sweet flag propagated?

Increase sweet flag by dividing the rhizomes (see page 36).

How do you recommend harvesting and drying sweet flag?

Sweet flag rhizomes should be dug in early fall. Dry them in the sun, preferably at 85° or 90° F., for several days.

Sweet flag: This grasslike perennial must be grown by water, or in very moist soil.

Sweet woodruff *(Galium odoratum;* formerly *Asperula odorata)*

How is sweet woodruff used?

A traditional beverage known as May wine is flavored with the leaves of sweet woodruff. To make May wine, fill a quart jar with fresh sweet woodruff leaves and pour enough Rhine wine over the leaves to fill the jar. Cover, refrigerate, and allow the mixture to steep for four weeks.

Although the fresh leaves are odorless, when dried they take on the scent of clover or new-mown hay and so are popular in sachets.

What garden conditions should I provide for sweet woodruff?

With its loose clusters of star-shaped, white flowers in late spring, this 6- to 8-inch plant makes a fine perennial ground cover, hardy through Zone 4. Give it an open, acid, rather moist soil, rich in organic matter. It must have good drainage, but it thrives in either shade or partial shade. It should not be fertilized.

Can I propagate sweet woodruff from seeds?

Germination is often poor, so it would be better to propagate by dividing plants in early to mid-spring when growth starts, or by rooting stem cuttings from new growth in late spring and summer.

When should sweet woodruff leaves be harvested?

The best time is in the spring before the plants flower. Dry them on a screen in a cool, dry, well-ventilated area.

Tansy *(Tanacetum vulgare)*

Is it true that tansy is a good insect repellent?

Yes. Strew fresh leaves on doorsteps to keep ants away, hang dried leaves and flowers in doorways to repel moths, and set live plants around the outside of the house to discourage a variety of insects from entering.

Does tansy have other uses?

Because it contains a poisonous drug, tansy may not be used for food or drink. With its fernlike foliage and clusters of buttonlike, bright yellow flowers on 4-foot stems, it is an attractive addition to the perennial flower or herb garden. It blooms in late summer and is hardy to Zone 3. The flowers are excellent in dried arrangements, and both flowers and leaves can be used in sachets and potpourri. The dried leaves and stems also make a natural dye.

What type of soil does tansy like?

Grow tansy in moist, well-drained soil, rich in organic matter. Fertilize each year in spring when growth starts.

I grew tansy last year, but it got very weedy. I wondered if it was in too sunny a spot?

Tansy spreads naturally and rapidly, and giving it less sun will only make it more leggy. Set new plants 12 to 18 inches apart, and insert an underground metal barrier around them to help keep them within bounds. You can also grow tansy in a container. Thin or cut tansy back every year.

How should I propagate tansy?

Divide tansy in either spring or fall—you'll find that any piece of root that has a bud eye will grow into a new plant. You can also grow tansy from seed. Start seeds indoors in mid-spring, or

Ann Reilly

outside in early spring as soon as the soil can be worked, sowing seeds ½ inch deep. Germination will take ten to fourteen days.

When should I pick tansy?

Cut the stems at ground level just before the flowers have fully opened. Hang the stems upside down and dry them in a dark, dry, well-ventilated place.

Tarragon *(Artemisia Dracunculus* var. *sativa)*

I have come across both tarragon and French tarragon in recipes. Are they the same thing?

The tarragon referred to in recipes is French tarragon. Russian or Siberian tarragon, for which you may find seeds, is a tasteless, invasive weed. French tarragon rarely flowers, and when it does produce an occasional yellow bloom, it does not set seed.

How can I recognize French tarragon when I buy plants?

Taste a little piece of a leaf. If it has a delicate licorice flavor, it is French tarragon. Tarragon is a woody perennial with dark green, linear leaves, and with the potential for growing 3 feet high.

How is tarragon used in cooking?

Tarragon is particularly nice with fish and chicken and in bearnaise sauce. Along with parsley, chives, and chervil, it is

Tarragon: The delicate, licoricelike flavor of tarragon is particularly suited to fish and chicken dishes.

one of the *fines herbes* used in French cooking. Like many culinary herbs, tarragon may be used dried but is much better fresh.

What kind of soil does tarragon need?

Almost any well-drained garden soil, rich in organic matter. Water when the soil starts to dry out. Roots must be dry during the winter or the plants will not survive. Fertilize with fish emulsion in early spring when growth starts and again in early summer, but do not use chemical fertilizer to force growth, as the quality of the leaves is adversely affected by a too-fertile diet.

Does tarragon need full sun?

It prefers full sun, but will endure light shade.

I tried to grow tarragon in Monterey, California, last year, but it did not do well. What is the problem?

It may not be cold enough during the winter. A true perennial, tarragon must have temperatures between 32° and -10° F. (Zones 5 to 8) during the winter. If you wish to grow tarragon where winters are mild, you can dig up plants and refrigerate them over the winter: Wash soil off the roots; prune the roots back so that they are about 2 inches long; place the entire plant in a plastic bag, fastened closed; and store in the hydrator for about six weeks.

Can tarragon be grown from seed?

As explained above, the culinary herb French tarragon does not set seed. To propagate, therefore, you must divide plants in early spring or take cuttings in summer. Space new plants 12 to 24 inches apart.

When should I pick tarragon leaves?

To use leaves fresh, pick them at any time. To dry them, pick leaves in the early fall and dry them on a screen or in a paper bag in a warm, dry, well-ventilated area. Handle the leaves carefully during picking and drying as they bruise easily and bruising causes them to lose their essential oil and flavor.

Thyme *(Thymus vulgaris)*

I have seen many different kinds of thyme. Which is the one used in cooking?

The best and most commonly used thyme for cooking is *T. vulgaris*. A spreading perennial, 6 to 12 inches tall with small, aromatic, gray-green leaves and clusters of lavender-blue flowers in spring and summer, thyme delicately flavors poultry stuffing, soups, egg, meat, and vegetable dishes. Bees that feed on its nectar produce a distinctive honey. Legend holds that thyme was one of the herbs used in Christ's manger.

What are some other thymes that I could use in my herb garden?

Two other popular culinary thymes are lemon thyme (*T. x citriodorus*), which has round, deliciously flavored leaves, and caraway thyme (*T. Herba-barona*), which has small leaves with a flavor similar to caraway. The ornamental or creeping thymes, such as mother-of-thyme (*T. praecox*), are aromatic and can be used in cooking, but they are not as tasty as *T. vulgaris*. All thymes are members of the Mint family.

I would like to grow thyme for seasoning. Will it stand our severe western New York winters?

In western New York, you are on the edge of thyme's winter hardiness limit, which is Zone 5. Protect it during the winter with a mulch of evergreen boughs or straw. The greatest menace to thyme during winter, however, is not so much the cold as it is the wetness caused by snow and poor drainage, which is apt to cause winterkill. One means of preventing this is to grow thyme on rather poor or sandy soil, containing gravel or screened cinders. Do not feed thyme in summer to force growth, and do not cut its tops after September 1. Try these ways of keeping plants dry during winter: Place them in a cold frame, cover them with boxes to help keep the snow off, and be certain that their position is well drained.

Thyme: Lemon thyme is a particularly popular culinary thyme.

Madelaine Gray

What are the best growing conditions for thyme?

Full sun in light, sandy, dry, well-drained soil. Fertilize very lightly in early spring with bonemeal or cottonseed meal. Prune back plants in spring or summer to encourage bushiness.

How can I increase my thyme plants?

The best culinary thymes are not easily propagated from seeds, so we recommend making divisions, taking cuttings, or layering. Other thymes may be started from seeds indoors in late winter through late spring; seeds will sprout in twenty-one to thirty days. Sow seeds outdoors in early spring as soon as the soil can be worked, ¼ to ½ inch deep. Divide established plants in early spring; take stem cuttings in summer. Set new plants 10 inches apart.

If I begin new plants by layering this summer, can I move them this fall?

To be certain that the roots are well developed, wait until the following spring.

When can thyme be harvested?

Whenever the plant is large enough to pick the leaves, up until the time the plant is in full bloom.

Valerian, Heliotrope *(Valeriana officinalis)*

Is valerian still used medicinally?

Although its roots were once used in medicines, valerian is now grown principally for its clusters of fragrant flowers in a perennial border. In addition, its roots, which have an unpleasant odor when fresh, seem to attract earthworms to the garden. Legend holds that because the roots were also thought to attract rats, the Pied Piper of Hamlin carried valerian. When dry, the roots lose their unpleasant odor and are used as a fixative in potpourri (see page 66).

Is valerian a perennial?

Yes, but when it is being grown for its roots, it is dug up in its second year. If you wish to grow some as perennials, harvest only what you need and save the rest for propagation for following years. Valerian is hardy through Zone 3.

I tried valerian two years ago for the first time. It was a pretty background for the rest of the garden, but it needed staking. Would fertilizer strengthen its stems?

Valerian grows 3 to 5 feet tall and normally needs to be supported in some way. Set plants 12 inches apart so that they can help to support each other. Fertilize in spring when growth starts but additional fertilizing will not help strengthen the stems.

What kind of soil does valerian need?

Valerian likes well-drained soil, rich in organic matter and constantly moist.

Will valerian grow in partial shade?

Yes, it does equally well in full sun or partial shade.

When does valerian bloom?

The flat to round clusters of white, pink, lavender, or blue flowers fill the garden with bloom from late spring to late summer.

I have not had luck growing valerian from seeds. Am I doing something wrong?

If your seeds are not fresh they will not germinate. Further, do not cover seeds, as they need light to germinate. Start seeds indoors except in the longest of growing seasons, because it takes twenty-one to twenty-five days for the seeds to germinate and ten to twelve weeks for a seedling to reach transplanting size. Move plants outdoors four weeks before the last spring frost, and set them 12 inches apart. Less time-consuming, divide plants in spring or fall.

When should valerian be harvested?

The flowers do not dry well, but they can be cut for fresh bouquets at any time. Dig roots in the fall of their second year before the first frost, wash all soil from them, split any that are larger than ¾ inch, and dry them in an oven at 120° F.

Watercress (*Nasturtium officinale*)

Does the botanical name of watercress, *Nasturtium officinale*, mean it is related to garden nasturtium?

No, they are not even in the same plant family, but they both have a pungent, peppery flavor and a somewhat similar appearance. Watercress is a biennial aquatic plant with thin, divided, round leaves and four-petaled flowers. It grows best in cold, running water at the edge of a clear, fresh stream.

Can I grow watercress in a garden without running water?

Yes, plants will last for a time in a moist, shady spot in the garden, but they will not live through the winter unless covered with water. They can also be grown in tubs, whiskey barrels, or other watertight containers. They become true perennials only when grown in running water that has an alkaline pH.

As an alternative, you can grow annual garden cress (*Lepidium sativum*), which will furnish salad greens in three to four weeks, or annual garden nasturtium, the leaves, flowers, or seeds of which may be used in salads. (Do *not* eat packaged nasturtium seeds, which may have been chemically treated.)

What are the uses of fresh watercress?

Use watercress in salads, in sandwiches, and as a garnish, or cook it with vegetables for a peppery flavor.

How should I grow watercress from seed?

Sow seeds in water or in a constantly wet medium that has a temperature of 55° F., and do not cover them. Germination will take seven to ten days. You can also divide watercress in spring or fall.

When should I harvest watercress?

If you allow some plants to flower, they will drop their seeds in late summer, giving you new plants to begin harvesting by late fall.

Wintergreen (*Gaultheria procumbens*)

How is wintergreen used?

Wintergreen is a 3-inch evergreen shrub, commonly seen as a ground cover in North American woods. It is a well-known flavor of commercial candy and chewing gum. The fresh-picked leaves lend a refreshing mint flavor to tea.

What soil does wintergreen require?

Wintergreen needs the soil typically found in the woods—rich, moist, acidic, and well drained. Fertilize plants in spring when growth starts, and keep them mulched with 2 to 4 inches of pine needles during the summer.

Can I grow wintergreen on a sunny slope?

No, wintergreen needs a site in partial to full shade.

Does wintergreen flower?

Yes. Small, white, bell-shaped, spring flowers are followed by red berries in fall.

Can I grow wintergreen from seeds?

Cuttings or layering are easier methods of propagation, but if you want to grow wintergreen from seeds, either sow the seeds outdoors in fall for germination the following spring, or place them in moistened peat moss in the refrigerator for three months. Germination may be slow.

Maggie Oster

Wintergreen: A true woodland plant, wintergreen requires a rich, moist, acidic, well-drained spot.

Can I dig a plant of wintergreen from the wild and move it into my garden?

You can, but small plants transplant most successfully. It is probably better to take cuttings or buy a plant at a nursery.

When should I root cuttings of wintergreen?

Root cuttings in early summer, using new growth. You can also propagate wintergreen by pinning outside branches to the ground. The newly rooted plants can be dug the following spring. Set plants 12 inches apart.

When can the leaves of wintergreen be harvested?

Harvest leaves at any time for fresh or dry use. Keep plants compact and shapely by pruning them in spring, and use the prunings fresh, or dry them on a screen in a cool, dry, airy place.

Winter savory *(Satureja montana)*

How do winter and summer savory differ?

Actually, they are quite similar, except that winter savory is a perennial, hardy through Zone 5, and summer savory is an annual. Both have the same uses and are grown in the same

Winter savory: Perennial winter savory should be pruned severely in early spring to encourage compact growth.

manner. To encourage compactness, severely prune winter savory in early spring when growth starts. It may need winter protection in cold climates. (See also summer savory, page 117.)

Are winter and summer savory propagated the same way?

Each can be propagated by seed and has the same germinating requirements, although winter savory may take a little longer to sprout. Winter savory can also be propagated by division in early spring or by layering during the summer. Plants will be rooted and ready to transplant the following spring. Set plants 12 to 15 inches apart.

Wormwood. See Artemisia

Yarrow (*Achillea Millefolium*)

Can you tell me about the history of yarrow?

The Latin name for yarrow, *Achillea*, stems from Achilles, who is said to have recognized its healing properties. Even during the

Yarrow: Formerly valued for its healing properties, yarrow is now used primarily in dried flower arrangements and in herbal bath products.

Ann Reilly

Elizabethan era soldiers carried it as a first-aid treatment for wounds. Today its primary use is for dried flower arrangements and herbal bath products.

Can I grow yarrow in a sunny flower garden?

With its fernlike foliage and clusters of pink, magenta, or white flowers, yarrow is an extremely attractive plant, which blossoms in early summer and again in fall if it is cut back after the first bloom. Flowering stems grow 2 to 3 feet tall over a clump of foliage at their base. It can be invasive, however, so grow it in a container or with an underground barrier around it, or be prepared to thin it out each year.

I have seen yarrow with yellow flowers. What is this plant?

Yellow yarrow (*A. filipendulina*) is a closely related species. Grown in the same manner as *A. millefolium*, it is a slightly taller plant, with slightly larger flower heads.

Can I grow yarrow in my south Florida garden?

Probably not. Yarrow is a perennial best grown in Zones 3 to 8, because it needs freezing temperatures during the winter.

What type of soil does yarrow prefer?

Yarrow likes a dry, acidic, well-drained soil with little organic matter. It needs little or no fertilizer, but it benefits from a light application of bonemeal in spring when growth starts.

If I start plants from seed, will they bloom the first year?

When started from seed, plants usually will not bloom until the second year, unless given a very early start indoors. Be sure not to cover the seed as it is very fine and needs light to germinate. Seeds will sprout in ten days. Outdoors, sow seeds from mid-spring to midsummer, and space seedlings to stand 8 to 12 inches apart.

When can I divide plants of yarrow?

Divide the plants in either early spring or early fall. Since yarrow will need thinning almost every year, the plants that are removed can be given to friends and neighbors or transplanted to another part of the garden.

When should I cut yarrow for drying?

Cut the flowering stems off at the base just before the plants are in full bloom. Hang the stems upside down in a warm, dark, dry place.

Characteristics of Favorite Herbs

NAME	ANNUAL/PERENNIAL	HEIGHT	PLANT PART USED	BASIC USES	PROPAGATION	EXPOSURE	SOIL
Angelica	B	5'	L,St,Se,R	Cu,D	S	S,LtSh	M
Anise	HA	18"-2'	L,Se	Cu	S	S	D
Anise hyssop	P	3'-4'	L	P	S,D,C	S,LtSh	D,A
Artemisia	P	2'-3'	L,F	F,I	S,D,C	S	D,A,M
Basil	TA	18"-2'	L	Cu	S	S	D
Bee balm	P	2'-4'	L	D	S,D,C	S,LtSh	D,A
Borage	HA	2'-3'	L,F	Cu,G	S	S,LtSh	D
Burnet	P	18"-2'	L	Cu,D	S,D	S	D
Calendula	HA	6"-2'	F	F,G,Cu,D,P	S	S,LtSh	M
Caraway	B	2'-30"	L,Se,R	Cu	S	S	D
Catnip	P	2'-4'	L	(see page 00)	S,D	S,PtSh	D
Chamomile (Roman)	P	6"	F	D,Co	S,C	S,LtSh	D,A,M
Chamomile (German)	HA	24"-30"	F	D	S	S,LtSh	D,A,M
Chervil	HA	2'	L	Cu	S	LtS,PtSh,Sh	M
Chives	P	8"-24"	L,F	Cu	S,D	S,LtSh	M
Clary sage	B	3'	F	F	S	S	M
Comfrey	P	2'-3'	R,L	(see page 00)	S,D	S,PtSh	A,M
Coriander	HA	30"	L,Se	Cu	S	S	M
Costmary	P	2'-3'	L	Cu	D,C	S,PtSh	D,A
Cumin	TA	6"	S	Cu	S	S	A
Dill	HA	2'-3'	L,Se	Cu	S	S	M
Fennel	P(A)	4'-5'	L,Se,St	Cu	S	S	D,A,M
Garlic	HA	3'	R	Cu	S,Cl	S	M
Germander	P	10"-12"	-	H	S,D,C	S,PtSh	D,A
Ginseng	P	15"-18"	R	D	S,C	Sh	M
Horehound	P	18"-24"	L,F	Cu,D	S,D,C	S	D,A
Horseradish	P	2'	R	Cu	C	S,PtSh	M
Hyssop	P	18"-24"	L,F	D,H	S,D,C	S,LtSh	D
Lavender	P	18"-24"	F	Cu,P,Co,I	S,C	S	D
Lavender cotton	P	18"-24"	L,F	P,H,I	S,D,C	S	D
Lemon balm	P	2'	L	D,Cu	S,D,C	LtSh	D,A,M
Lemon grass	P(A)	6'	L	Cu,D,P	D	S	M
Lemon verbena	P(A)	3'	L	P	C	S	M
Lovage	P	3'	L,Se,St	Cu	S,D	S,LtSh	M
Marjoram	P(A)	8"-10"	L	Cu	S,C	S	A
Mint	P	12"-18"	L	Cu,D	S,D,C	S,LtSh	A,M
Oregano	P,A	18"-24"	L	Cu	S,D,C	S	A
Parsley	B(A)	8"-12"	L	Cu,G	S	S,LtSh	A
Pennyroyal (American)	HA	1'	L	P,I	S	S,LtSh	M
Pennyroyal (English)	P	6"	L	P,I	D,C	S,LtSh	M
Perilla	P(A)	18"-36"	L,F	Cu	S	S,LtSh	D
Rosemary	P(A)	1'-5'	L	Cu,Co	S,D,C,L	S,PtSh	A

Characteristics of Favorite Herbs

NAME	ANNUAL/ PERENNIAL	HEIGHT	PLANT PART USED	BASIC USES	PROPAGATION	EXPOSURE	SOIL
Rue	P	18″-36″	L	H,I	S,D,C	S	M
Safflower	TA	3′	F	Cu,P,F	S	S	A
Saffron	P	6″-8″	F	Cu	Co	S,LtSh	M
Sage	P	18″-24″	L	Cu,D	S,D,C	S,LtSh	A,M
Scented geraniums	P(A)	1′-4′	L	Cu,D,P	S,C	S	A
Sesame	TA	2′-3′	S	Cu	S	S	A
Summer savory	HA	12″-18″	L	Cu	S	S	M
Sweet cicely	P	2′	L,Se,St	Cu,D	S,C	Sh	M
Sweet flag	P	18″-6′	R	P	D	S,PtSh	M
Sweet woodruff	P	6″-8″	L	D,P	D,C	PtSh,Sh	M
Tansy	P	4′	L,F	F,I,P	S,D	S	M
Tarragon	P	3′	L	Cu	D,C	S,LtSh	A
Thyme	P	6″-12″	L	Cu	S,D,C,L	S	D
Valerian	P	3′-5′	R,F	P	S,D	S,PtSh	M
Watercress	B	3′	L	Cu,G	S,D	Sh	M
Wintergreen	P	3″	L	D	S,C,L	PtSh, Sh	M
Winter savory	P	6″-12″	L	Cu	S,D,L	S	M
Yarrow	P	2′-3′	F	F,Co	S,D	S	D

Plant Type: P = Perennial
                 P(A) = Perennial grown as an annual
                 B = Biennial
                 B(A) = Biennial grown as an annual
                 HA = Hardy Annual
                 TA = Tender Annual

Plant Part Used: L = Leaves
                      F = Flowers
                      R = Roots
                      Se = Seeds
                      St = Stem

Basic Uses: Co = Cosmetic
              Cu = Culinary
              D = Drinks, hot or cold
              F = Dried flower
              G = Garnish
              H = Hedge
              I = Insect Repellent
              P = Potpourri

Method of Propagation: S = Seeds
                          C = Cuttings
                          Cl = Clove
                          Co = Corm
                          D = Division
                          L = Layering

Exposure: S = Sun
            LtSh = Light Shade
            PtSh = Part Shade
            Sh = Shade

Soil: D = Dry
       A = Average
       M = Moist

Germination Time and Plant Spacing

HERB	GERMINATION TIME (in days)	PLANT SPACING
Angelica	21-25*	3 feet
Anise	20-28	6-9 inches
Anise hyssop	7-10	1½ feet
Artemisia	7-10	2-4 feet
Basil	7-10	1 foot
Bee balm	15-20	1 foot
Borage	7-10*	1 foot
Burnet	8-10	15 inches
Calendula	10-14	12-15 inches
Caraway	10-14*	6-9 inches
Catnip	7-10	1½-2 feet
Chamomile (Roman)	7-10	3-4 inches
Chamomile (German)	7-10	8 inches
Chervil	7-14*	6-8 inches
Chives	10-14	6-8 inches
Clary	14-21*	1 foot
Comfrey	7-10*	3 feet
Coriander	10-14	8-10 inches
Costmary	not grown from seed	3 feet
Cumin	10-14	6 inches
Dill	21-25	4-8 inches
Fennel	10-14	8-12 inches
Garlic	10-14	3-4 inches
Germander	25-30	1 foot
Ginseng	*	15 inches
Horehound	10-14	8-10 inches
Horseradish	not grown from seed	1 foot
Hyssop	7-10*	12-18 inches
Lavender	20-40*	1 foot
Lavender cotton	15-20	1½ feet
Lemon balm	14	1½ feet

Germination Time and Plant Spacing

HERB	GERMINATION TIME (in days)	PLANT SPACING
Lemon grass	not grown from seed	3 feet
Lemon verbena	not grown from seed	2-5 feet
Lovage	10-14	12-15 inches
Marjoram	8-14	6-8 inches
Mint	12-16	1-2 feet
Oregano	10-15	1 foot
Parsley	14-21	6-8 inches
Pennyroyal (American)	15	1-2 feet
Pennyroyal (English)	not grown from seed	1-2 feet
Perilla	15-20	1-1½ feet
Rosemary	18-21	1-1½ feet
Rue	10-14	6-12 inches
Safflower	10	1 foot
Saffron	not grown from seed	3-4 inches
Sage	14-21	1-1½ feet
Scented geranium	20-50	1-2 feet
Sesame	5-7	6 inches
Summer savory	10-15	4-6 inches
Sweet cicely	30 + *	2 feet
Sweet flag	not grown from seed	1-3 feet
Sweet woodruff	not grown from seed	1-1½ feet
Tansy	10-14	1-1½ feet
Tarragon	not grown from seed	1-2 feet
Thyme	21-30	10 inches
Valerian	21-25	1 foot
Watercress	7-10	12-15 inches
Wintergreen	30 +	1 foot
Winter savory	15-20	12-15 inches
Yarrow	10	8-12 inches

*Sow in the fall for spring germination

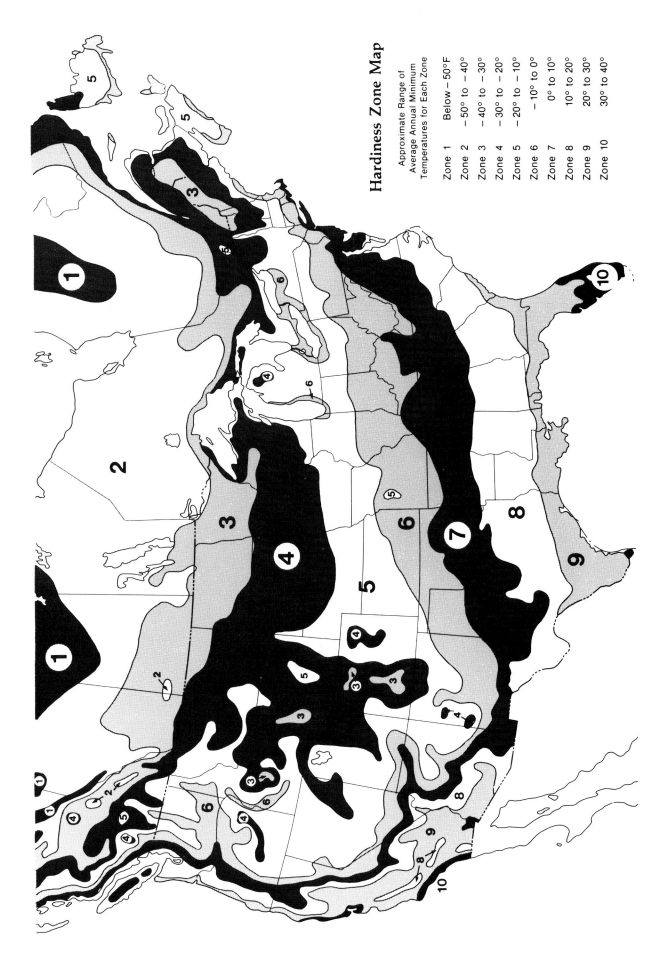

Hardiness Zone Map

Approximate Range of
Average Annual Minimum
Temperatures for Each Zone

Zone 1   Below −50°F
Zone 2   −50° to −40°
Zone 3   −40° to −30°
Zone 4   −30° to −20°
Zone 5   −20° to −10°
Zone 6   −10° to 0°
Zone 7   0° to 10°
Zone 8   10° to 20°
Zone 9   20° to 30°
Zone 10   30° to 40°

Glossary

ANNUAL. A plant that is sown, flowers, sets seeds, and dies all within one season.

BACILLUS POPILLIA. Milky spore disease, a bacterium that infects Japanese beetles.

BACILLUS THURINGIENSIS (BT). A bacterium that causes disease in a variety of pest larvae, but is safe to humans, birds and pets, and plants; marketed under such tradenames as Biotrol, Dipel, and Thuricide.

BED. A planting that is accessible from all sides and intended to be viewed from all sides.

BIENNIAL. A plant that takes two years to complete its growing cycle from seed; usually flowers, fruits, and dies during its second season.

BORDER. A planting at the edge of an area.

BROADCAST. Scatter seeds freely over the entire seedbed.

COMPOST. A rich, porous mixture composed of decaying or decayed organic matter.

CORM. A modified, swollen stem filled with food storage tissue; a fleshy root similar to a bulb, but not solid.

COTYLEDONS. The first, or seed leaves; food storage cells, not true leaves.

CULTIVAR. A cultivated variety, usually unique and an improvement in the species, created by the successful cross-pollination of two different plants within a species.

CUTTING. A method of plant propagation whereby a piece of plant is cut from a parent plant and inserted into a growing medium to encourage root development, thus forming a new plant.

DAMPING OFF. A fungus disease carried in unsterile soil; causes young seedlings to wither and die.

DIVISION. A method of plant propagation whereby a plant (including its root system) is dug and cut or pulled apart; the resulting plants can be replanted.

ESSENTIAL OIL. The result of a distillation process that extracts the oil containing the distinctive aroma of a plant (or animal).

FINES HERBES. An herb mixture used in French cooking; traditionally consists of chives, chervil, parsley, and tarragon, but sometimes contains a variety of additional herbs as well.

FIXATIVE. A material, such as angelica root, benzoin and gum storax, calamus root, orrisroot, and sandalwood, that aids in preserving the leaves and petals, as well as the natural scent, of a plant.

FLAT. A shallow, topless box with drainage holes in the bottom; used for germinating seeds, growing young transplants, or propagating cuttings.

GERMINATION. The sprouting of seeds.

HARDENING OFF. The process of subjecting seedlings that were begun indoors to increasing amounts of light and outdoor temperatures prior to transplanting them into the garden.

HARDINESS ZONES. U.S. Department of Agriculture classifications according to annual minimum temperatures and/or lengths of growing seasons. *See* zone map, page 134.

HARDY ANNUAL. An annual plant that withstands frost and thus can be planted outdoors in early spring or left out late into fall.

HERB. A plant that dies down over winter rather than forming woody stems; a plant valued for its medicinal, flavorful, or aromatic qualities.

HOT CAP. A plastic or paper tent made to protect young plants from wind and cold.

KITCHEN GARDEN. A fairly small garden composed of edible plants, both vegetable and herb.

KNOT GARDEN. A traditional garden consisting of low-growing herbs planted in a formal, intricate design that resembles knotted ropes.

LAYERING. A method of plant propagation whereby a long, flexible stem of a woody plant is secured to, or slightly under, the ground to encourage root development at the point of contact with the ground, thus forming a new plant.

LEAF MOLD. Decayed leaves.

LOAM. A soil consisting of about a 50-50 mixture of sand and clay.

MULCH. A protective covering, such as bark chips or sawdust, spread over the ground to reduce evaporation, maintain an even soil temperature, prevent erosion, control weeds, and enrich the soil.

NPK. Chemical symbols representing nitrogen, phosphorus, and potassium, respectively; the primary ingredients in most lawn and garden fertilizers.

NITROGEN. One of the three most important plant nutrients, an essential element of chlorophyll; stunted growth and pale yellow foliage indicate nitrogen deficiency. *See also* Phosphorus; Potassium.

PEAT MOSS. Compacted plant debris, including sphagnum moss.

PERENNIAL. A plant that lives from year to year, usually flowering and setting seed in spring and summer, dying to the ground in winter, and regrowing the following spring.

pH. The relative acidity and alkalinity of a soil on a scale of 1 to 14; a soil with a pH of 7 is considered neutral.

PHOSPHORUS. One of the three most important plant nutrients, essential for good root and stem development; stunted growth and purple coloring of leaves and stems indicate phosphorus deficiency. *See also* Nitrogen; Potassium.

PINCHING BACK. The technique of pinching out the growing tip of developing plants in order to encourage bushiness.

POTASSIUM. One of the three most important plant nutrients; slow growth, high incidence of disease, and bronzing of leaves indicate potassium deficiency. *See also* Nitrogen; Phosphorus.

POTPOURRI. A mixture, usually consisting of flowers, leaves, essential oils, and spices, combined with a fixative to preserve fragrance.

PROPAGATION. Multiplying plants by one of a variety of techniques. *See also* Cutting; Division; Layering.

SEEDLING. A young plant grown from seed.

SET OUT. Plant.

SILICA GEL. A desiccant used to dry herb flowers for craft use.

SLOW-RELEASE FERTILIZER. A fertilizer formulated to be inactive until released by water or temperature and to activate slowly over a period of time (e.g., 3-month or 6-month formulations).

SOIL AMENDMENTS. Ingredients such as sand, peat moss, or compost that are added to soil to improve its texture.

SPECIES. The basic division of the living world, consisting of distinct and similar individuals that can breed together to produce offspring similar to themselves.

STRATIFICATION. A technique that involves chilling moistened seeds for a period of time prior to planting them.

SUCCESSION PLANTING. Sowing seeds of a specific plant every one to two weeks over a period of time in order to have a continuous supply.

TAMPER. A tool similar to a mason's float; used for tamping soil firmly in flats when sowing seed.

TENDER ANNUAL. A plant that is easily injured by frost and must be planted only after the ground has warmed up.

VARIETY. A plant that is different from the true species occurring in nature.

VERMICULITE. Lightweight, highly water-absorbent material resulting from the expansion of mica granules under high temperatures; used in potting medium.

VOLUNTEER. A seedling that springs up from seeds that were dropped and left in the ground from the year before.

WINTER HARDY. Able to withstand frost.

Appendix

Atlanta Botanical Garden
Piedmont Park at South Prado
Atlanta, GA 30309
(404) 876-5858
Fee, Tuesday-Sunday; children
   under 6 free

Berkshire Garden Center
Routes 102 and 183
Stockbridge, MA 01262
(413) 298-3926

Boerner Botanical Gardens
Whitnall Park
5879 South 92nd Street
Hales Corners, WI 53130
(414) 425-1132

Brooklyn Botanic Garden
1000 Washington Avenue
Brooklyn, NY 11225
(212) 622-4433

Chicago Botanic Garden
Glencoe Road
Glencoe, IL 60022
(312) 835-5440
Parking fee

Colonial Williamsburg
Williamsburg, VA 23185
(804) 229-1000 (ext. 2751)
Fee

Denver Botanical Gardens
909 York Street
Denver, CO 80206
(303) 575-2547

Dow Gardens
1018 West Main Street
Midland, MI 48640
(517) 631-2677

Farmington Museum House
37 High Street
Farmington, CT 06032
(203) 677-9222
Fee

Filoli Center
Canada Road
Woodside, CA 94062
(415) 364-2880
Fee; no children under 12

Gilbertie's Herb Gardens
Sylvan Lane
Westport, CT 06880
(203) 227-4175

Hancock Shaker Village
Pittsfield, MA 01202
(413) 443-0188
Fee

Huntington Botanical Gardens
1151 Oxford Road
San Marino, CA 91108
(818) 449-3901

HERB GARDENS YOU CAN VISIT

Indiana Botanic Garden
636 177th Street
Hammond, IN 46324
(219) 931-2480

Kanapaha Botanical Gardens
4625 SW 63rd Boulevard
Gainesville, FL 32608
(904) 372-4981

Los Angeles State and County
Arboretum
301 North Baldwin Avenue
Arcadia, CA 91006
(213) 446-8251

Morton Arboretum
Rte. 53 and East-West Tollway
Lisle, IL 60532
(312) 968-0074
Fee

Mount Vernon
Mount Vernon Memorial
Parkway
Mount Vernon, VA 22121
(703) 780-2000
Fee

New York Botanical Garden
Bronx Park, 1 East 200th Street
Bronx, NY 10458
(212) 220-8728
Fee

Old Sturbridge Village
Sturbridge, MA 01566
(617) 347-3362
Fee

Plimoth Plantation
P.O. Box 1620
Plymouth, MA 02360
(508) 746-1622

Queens Botanical Garden
43-50 Main Street
Flushing, NY 11568
(212) 886-3800

Robison York State Herb Garden
Cornell Plantations
1 Plantations Road
Ithaca, NY 14850
(607) 256-3020

J. Paul Getty Museum and
Gardens
17985 Pacific Coast Highway
Malibu, CA 90265
(213) 459-8402

National Herb Garden
National Arboretum
3501 New York Avenue NE
Washington, DC 20002
(202) 475-4815

Western Reserve Herb Society
Garden
Greater Cleveland Garden
Center
11030 East Boulevard
Cleveland, OH 44106
(216) 721-1600

SUPPLIERS OF HERB SEEDS AND PLANTS

Ahrens Nursery and Plant Labs
Route 1
Huntingburg, IN 47542
(812) 683-3055

Caprilands Herb Farm
534 Silver Street
Coventry, CT 06238
(203) 742-7244
Catalog, send self-addressed,
stamped envelope

Carroll Gardens
P.O. Box 310
Westminster, MD 21157
(301) 848-5422
Catalog, $2

Catnip Acres Herb Farm
67 Christian Street
Oxford, CT 06483
(203) 888-5649

Fox Hill Farm
444 West Michigan Avenue,
Box 9
Parma, MI 49269-0009
(517) 531-3179
Catalog, $1

Goodwin Creek Gardens
P.O. Box 83
Williams, OR 97544
(503) 846-7357 Catalog, $1

J.L. Hudson, Seedsman
P.O. Box 1058
Redwood City, CA 94064
Catalog, $1 (no phone orders)

Johnny's Selected Seeds
299 Foss Hill Road
Albion, ME 04910
(207) 437-9294

Le Jardin du Gourmet
West Danville, VT 05873
(no phone orders)

Lost Prairie Herb Farm
805 Kienas Road
Kalispell, MT 59901
(406) 756-7742
Catalog, $1

Meadowsweet Herb Farm
729 Mount Holly Road
Shrewsbury, VT 05738
(802) 492-3565

Merry Gardens
P.O. Box 595
Camden, ME 04843
(207) 236-9064
Catalog, $2

Nichols Garden Nursery
1190 North Pacific Highway
Albany, OR 97321
(503) 928-9280

George W. Park Seed Co.
Cokesbury Road, Box 31
Greenwood, SC 29647-0001
(803) 223-7333

Richters
Goodwood, Ontario L0C 1A0
Canada
(416) 640-6677
Catalog, $2

Sandy Mush Herb Nursery
Route 2, Surrett Cove Road
Leicester, NC 28748
(704) 683-2014
Catalog, $4, deductible from
    first order

Taylor's Herb Garden
1535 Lone Oak Road
Vista, CA 92084
(619) 727-3485
Catalog, $1

HERB MAGAZINES AND NEWSLETTERS

The Business of Herbs
Northwind Farm Publications
Route 2, Box 246
Shevlin, MN 56676
(brochure available)

The Herb Companion
306 North Washington
Loveland, CO 80537

The Herb Quarterly Magazine
P.O. Box 548
Boiling Spring, PA 17007

The Herbal Thymes
39 Reed Street
Marcellus, NY 13108

Herban Lifestyles
84 Carpenter Road
New Hartford, CT 06057

International Herb Growers and
    Marketers Association
P.O. Box 281
Silver Spring, MD 17575

Potpourri from Herbal Acres
Box 428
Washington Crossing, PA 18977

Sage Advice
Box 626
Trumansburg, NY 14886

FURTHER READING

Culinary Herbs. Brooklyn Botanic Garden, 1982.

Duff, Gail. *Natural Fragrances: Outdoor Scents for Indoor Uses.* Garden Way Publishing, 1989

Foster, Gertrude, and Rosemary F. Louden. *Success with Herbs.* George W. Park Seed Co. (Greenwood, SC), 1980.

Foster, Steven. *Herbal Bounty: The Gentle Art of Herb Cultivation.* Gibbs M. Smith, Inc., 1984.

Gilbertie, Sal. *Herb Gardening at Its Best.* Atheneum, 1978.

Growing Herbs and Plants for Dyeing. Select Books, 1982.

Herbs: How to Grow. Sunset-Lane, 1972.

Herbs and Their Ornamental Uses. Brooklyn Botanic Garden, 1972.

Jacobs, Betty E. M. *Growing and Using Herbs Successfully.* Garden Way Publishing, 1981.

Lathrop, Norma. *Herbs: How to Select, Grow, and Enjoy.* HP Books, 1981.

Marcin, Marietta Marshall. *The Complete Book of Herbal Teas.* Congdon & Weed, 1983.

Paterson, Allen. *Herbs in the Garden.* J. M. Dent, 1985.

Shaudys, Phyllis. *The Pleasure of Herbs.* Garden Way Publishing, 1986.

The World of Herbs and Spices. Ortho Books, 1979.

Index